Me and My 15 Housemaids

A Journey of Self-Discovery Through Madness.

Fereshte (Shila) Gholamalizaden Kasbakhy

Me and My 15 Housemaids
Copyright © 2021 Fereshte Gholamalizaden Kasbakhy
First published in 2021

Hardcase: 978-1-922456-57-1
Paperback: 978-1-922456-58-8
E-book: 978-1-922456-59-5

Floral divider on pages 15 and 16 designed by Freepik.

All rights reserved. No part of this book may be reproduced, stored in a retrieval system, or transmitted by any means (electronic, mechanical, photocopying, recording, or otherwise) without written permission from the author.

Because of the dynamic nature of the Internet, any web addresses or links contained in this book may have changed since publication and may no longer be valid. The information in this book is based on the author's experiences and opinions. The views expressed in this book are solely those of the author and do not necessarily reflect the views of the publisher; the publisher hereby disclaims any responsibility for them.

The author of this book does not dispense any form of medical, legal, financial, or technical advice either directly or indirectly. The intent of the author is solely to provide information of a general nature to help you in your quest for personal development and growth. In the event you use any of the information in this book, the author and the publisher assume no responsibility for your actions. If any form of expert assistance is required, the services of a competent professional should be sought.

Publishing information

Publishing, design, and production facilitated by Passionpreneur Publishing,
A division of Passionpreneur Organization Pty Ltd
ABN: 48640637529

www.PassionpreneurPublishing.com
Melbourne, VIC | Australia

Testimonials

I attended 2 Interuniversal mysticism courses with Fereshte and found them fascinating. Very similar to meditation, the classes allow you time to disconnect from daily activities and gain perspective and a better understanding of yourself on a spiritual level. I thoroughly enjoyed the classes and found the sessions relaxing and very interesting, and Fereshte has a unique way to explain things to you to allow you to maximise on the benefits of this knowledge.

> **— Dima Al Sharif, Founder & CEO MOONEH LLC**
> **Author of Plated Heirlooms**

I met Fereshte at a very critical time in my life, her knowledge, professionalism and care allowed me to overcome by applying Faradarmani's beyond healing theory. A great mentor on my soul salvation path.

> **— Larissa Redaelli, Author of Happydemic**

Table of Contents

Acknowledgements	9
Introduction	11
Father	17
Mother	21
Rebecca	29
Moved	65
Moved Again	113
The Fall	139
The Rise	181
About the Author	225

Dedication

To my dear husband and my two beautiful sons who have always been my ultimate reasons for wanting to know more in this life.

Acknowledgements

My special thanks go to:

My dear sister Shirin, whose assistance was vital in the early stages of organising the manuscript of this book, and for her unconditional love and support throughout my life.

My dear friend Arezoo, for all the love, support and laughters.

My dear friend, Minoosh, whose love and support has been vital beyond description in my life.

My dear friend, Aida, for all our laughter and the philosophical discussions we had by the sea for several years and for boosting my confidence by being my very first student eleven years ago.

Introduction

Introduction

Most of us live our lives, day by day, with all our busy-ness, running mostly on auto-pilot. We think and do things in a certain manner because of the way we were taught by our surroundings and also because that is what we have seen being done, without knowing why and without even questioning our way of thinking and doing.

Most of us live our lives in this way for a long time, until life's circumstances push us toward the verge of breakdown. Only then might we realise that just thinking and doing things on auto-pilot will not cut it anymore.

This is Rebecca's journey through her life's ups and downs, portraying events that could be happening in the life of any person who is deeply in the grip of unconscious doing due to all the conditioning of the mind.

The road of self-discovery opens up for Rebecca as she finds herself on the cliff-edge of insanity, and that takes her to many unknown places, to many beginnings of all beginnings.

One day, we will all know the answers to all our questions, and that day, we will all only say one thing.

I wish I knew all this earlier, but as the famous saying offers,

Better late than never...

In the name of the Nameless,
Come and let's start
Sit through the night and let's appear, rise up like the sun in the morning
Doesn't matter how, in what manner and in what way!
Come and let's be awakened with a simple "flick" of intent

— **Dr. Mohammad Ali Taheri**

Introduction

I see an endless field, going on forever
I see the seeing behind all seeing
I am that, the vastest of the vast, the indescribable, the nearest of all
I hear the whispering of the Melody of Silence
I am The Melody Whisperer
I am The Hearing Whisperer
I am the Feeling Whisperer
I am the Seeing Whisperer
I am the Silence Whisperer

I hear the music in the background
> *The fragrance of that surrounding*
> *Face to Face and Eye to Eye*
> *The unique and the Indescribable*

Seeing a woman with long hair, dressed in a long, white, silky dress with pink linings.
Seeing a man with long gray hair, in a long, white, silky, dress with blue linings.
I see the Whispering of Their Dance together
I see the Whispering of The Silence around their dance
I hear the Whispering of No Silence
I feel the Whispering of The Love and Joy
I see the Whispering of The Oneness
I see the Whispering of The Whispering of I am
The Whispering of Perfection
The Whispering of Togetherness
The Whispering of Appearing
The Whispering of Disappearing

The Whispering of Being
The Whispering of Perfection
The Whispering of forever
I hear the song,
> *In your absence*
> *Worshiping your every single glance*
> *And awaiting the sweet return*
> *Drunk with love when with me*
> *With you, free from pain*
> *I wish, I am imprisoned in Seeing*
> *How to forget?*
> *The whole of me,*
> *That, that can't be forgotten*
> *All the hurt of not knowing*

I am seeing the whisper of a tree:
> "Taste!"

The two dancers stop!
Looking somehow naughty, smilingly, she picks a fruit, walks away without looking back, lays down in a green meadow and falls asleep.
The Whisperer of Silence Whispers,
> "Dream all you want!
> I Am the Whisperer of No Time.
> I Am the whisperer of No Place.
> You are the Whisperer of the Dreams.
> I Am the Whisperer of Patience."

Father

Father

I am seven or eight years old, not sure, when one morning, my dad wakes me up by yelling my name from our little front yard. "Time to be a man," he says. "Come with me. We are going somewhere!"

I am very happy that I don't need to stay at home and help mother with washing the dishes and buying groceries and all those womanly things. I walk with my dad, holding his hand, looking at him from time to time.

I like my dad. He is always kind to me. He smells like tobacco all the time though, and he coughs almost non-stop. We take a taxi to the main bazaar, and my dad introduces me to a friend of his who owns a household goods shop in that *bazaar*.

I am supposed to stay here and learn how to manage the store and the customers.

"Can he go to the bathroom by himself?" the shop owner asks.

Everyone in the store laughs along. I laugh too, because, well, everybody else is laughing. Meanwhile, deeply embarrassed, I think to myself, "What does he mean? Of course, I can go to the bathroom by myself. Am I too young to work?"

Dad leaves me there, and, as perky as I am, I do whatever is asked of me. I am happy that I am a man of the house now, earning money and all. My dad has been suffering from tuberculosis and isn't really allowed to work anywhere anymore.

A big van arrives. I am supposed to load off the supply for the store. I lift boxes that are twice the size of my body, and, in between, I also run to bring tea for the owner and his visiting friends or customers.

By six in the evening, when the shop closes, I head home. I walk back, since it is only a one-hour walk, thinking, "I'm starving! It would be so nice to eat something now."

When I get home, mother is still at work, and my three sisters are also waiting for her to come home and make something. Oh, the hunger. But since I am now a working man, I wait for mother to come home and serve us.

Come morning, I set out for the store. That done, I also work as a helper boy in the house of the owner. I help with all the household chores, including the preparation of the kebab and the serving of it every night.

Every day, when I see them having fun during their nightly gathering, I dream about having a family of my own someday and promise myself, "I will provide for everything, so my children will never have to work at a young age."

Mother

She is chasing me! I know it is going to hurt badly this time too, just like the other times. So I run, as if my life depends on it. But God, she is faster than I.

She tries a couple of times to grab the corner of my long-sleeved dress, but I, too, am fast and keep slipping through her fingers.

Finally, though, she catches up and grabs me. I fall on the grass in the rice farm, face down. My mouth is full of the soft soil and I am trying to spit it out and, at the same time, to keep her hands off me.

Mom, of course, is way bigger than I am, and as my twelve-year-old body gives in, she manages to put one of her feet over my neck.

"Mom, please!"

Tears roll down my cheeks, and, while still busy spitting the soil out of my mouth, I try to look into her eyes, hoping that maybe I can make her feel sorry for me and make her stop.

This time, though, her eyes have turned into something I've never seen before, not even in her.

They are blank and red at the same time, and the hate and anger emanating from them sends chills of fear through my whole body. It is almost as if she is determined to kill me this time. I truly think that this is it—I am going to die!

While trying to use her maximum power to break my neck with her foot, with her teeth biting together, she screams, "I told you not to touch the thin bread in the pantry, you ungrateful, ugly, miserable little rat!"

"I'm sorry, mom! I promise I'll never again make a mistake like this!" I say it half-choking, half-squeaking, trying to avoid looking at her burning eyes—there is something too intense in them. Instead, I try to look at the blue sky above her head.

Suddenly, she takes her foot off my neck and says, "I wish I never had you!"

I'm not sure if it is the foot or the words, but it takes a while before I can stand up. I am still looking at the blue sky as I touch my neck to see if all this pain is accompanied by any open sores, or worse, blood.

My chest, neck and back are aching. I continue to lay on the ground, staring at the blue sky above. I am trying not to change my position, as every tiny movement is followed by excruciating pain, mostly around my neck.

Completely shattered and lonely, with no one there to see what happened to me and nobody there to defend me, tears rolling down my cheeks, I somehow sit up and look around. All I can see is the rice farm, full of tall, golden rice stalks, ready for harvest. I see my older brothers far away from where I am, busy, working away in the rice farm.

I wish my sister were here, as I lay down again—out of exhaustion or hurt, I don't know—on the bare, muddy ground, shedding tears and thinking, "One day when I have children, I will be kind to them."

I don't know when, but I fall asleep on that cold, yet embracing, ground.

Him and I

Our eyes meet in a café. It is love at first sight. Soon we are married.

My In-laws

I have seven sisters-in-law. I live with five of them—who still aren't married—in one house, with my mother and father-in-law.

Every now and then, they keep telling me, "You are so long, don't stand next to us! Ah, you are so long!"

I feel inadequate when I'm with them. I wish I wasn't so tall and that they wouldn't call me 'long.' They are all shorter. I guess it's good to be short.

A Wedding Party

We are all ready to go to a wedding, all dressed up, and what I see makes my jaw drop. They are all wearing high heels!

Oh my God! It's good to be tall, but they make *me* feel bad about it. They actually secretly wish they could be as tall as me, and they have been making fun of me, making me feel bad about myself, all this while!

They think I'm dumb! I don't like these people.

After Four Years

We, finally, have managed to buy our own house. It is a fifteen-minute walk away from all my in-laws. By now, I have two beautiful daughters, ages three and one.

Pregnant Again

"Oh my God! What am I hearing? Oh, dear God, let this one not be a girl again. A boy is all I need to shut my in-laws up!"

I visit my husband's great aunt, and as we are having our afternoon tea and sweets, I hear my sisters-in-law whispering to one another, "If this one is also a girl, she should give it away to our older cousin. The poor guy can't have children of his own."

I find this to be very strange! They aren't even pretending to be classy or making an attempt to whisper so that I wouldn't hear what they are saying. Or maybe they are speaking loud enough on purpose.

I freak out, thinking, "Oh my God! They are thinking of taking my baby away from me if it's a girl. What am I going to do?!"

Going to sleep with all these worrying thoughts racing through my head, I wake up several times in the night. I feel a growing pain, on and off. I wait until my husband is up and has eaten his breakfast before I tell him that it's time for our third's arrival.

Almost six o'clock in the morning. I can't take this pain anymore, and I can't wait to see if my next baby is a boy.

Seeing me in pain, he hurries to go and look for a deliverer who lives nearby. My brother comes into the room and sees that I'm in the full-blown, active pain of labour. He questions, "Why are you alone?"

I say, "He is out to bring the lady labourer."

"Does your husband leave you like this?" and then, he leaves the room as well.

After ten minutes, my husband comes back with the lady deliverer and leaves for work right away.

~~~~

Finally, after two hours, I deliver.

The deliverer says happily, while holding the baby up, "It's a girl!"

My two older daughters are awake by now, playing with their toys and drinking their milk. The deliverer leaves after one hour. It's almost lunchtime soon. I'm thinking, "He is going to come home for lunch. I'd better prepare something for him. I hope he won't be upset. I hope he will still love me when he finds out that our number three is a girl too."

While taking the few, painful, steps toward the kitchen, I'm thinking, "I won't be able to do a thing if he decides to give my baby away. I hope he doesn't let them take my baby!"

Twelve o'clock sharp, he is home, and the lunch is ready.

He seems happy and says, "This baby brought luck for me, I made extra money today."

I am very happy that he is in a good mood. After lunch and his usual afternoon nap, he leaves for work again.

During That Day

The baby is burning with high fever, and I'm so worried that she might die. All I can think about is that I have to do all I can to save her so my in-laws won't think and start talking nonsense like this, "See! She can't even take care of her new baby, and yet, she refuses to give her away so someone else, who can't have a child, can be happy."

After I finish serving dinner to my two brothers, who've been living with us for the last three months, my husband comes home. After he is done with his dinner, I dare to say, "I need to tell you something!"

And before I can say anything else, I burst into tears. I can't control my crying. Shocked and upset by what he's seeing, he asks in a worried tone, "What's wrong? Is everything ok? Is everything ok with the baby?"

I cry even louder when I hear the word 'baby.' In a choppy voice and with my head down, terrified of any possible unfavourable response from him, I say, "The baby has high fever, but I think she will be ok. I'm upset because your sisters keep telling me that we have to give our baby girl to your old cousin who can't have a child."

And finally, I dare to look up into his eyes to detect his response.

I see that fierce look in his eyes, when he gets really mad, but I don't know what to think right at this moment. Is he upset because he thinks I shouldn't be bothering him with this nonsense, or…?

Suddenly, he drops his fork down, picks up the phone and dials. He starts yelling at his younger sister who picks up the phone and tells her to tell all the other sisters and his cousin to go to hell if they ever think they can speak about what should happen with my children.

The second call, I easily guess, is to the childless cousin.

Without saying hello to his cousin, he yells, "Over my dead body will you be able to take care of my daughter. I would not even let a dog be raised by you, let alone my daughter…"

Rebecca

Three

I'm only three years old. I can see mom and dad are crying. They have just come back from the hospital, where a doctor has done something called a surgery on my little brother.

They are crying because the doctor took out his left eye. There was no way other than taking the eye out, they said. An infection had destroyed the eye of my nine-month-old baby brother beyond repair.

Five

It is the middle of the night, and something wakes me up. I'm five. I feel something moving under my bed. I am terrified. I can't bring myself to look and see what it is. An uneasy feeling spreads all over my whole body. Scared, I wake my mother up.

I lie, "My tummy hurts!"

My mother gets up and walks to the kitchen. I follow her. I want to tell that I'm just scared. I want to tell her that I don't have any pain anywhere. Instead, I stand there quietly, waiting for whatever my mom is making for me.

She looks very sleepy and, with her eyes almost closed, she fixes me her magical cup of tea with crystal sugar. I feel comforted and happy that I'm with my mom. The thought of that 'thing' moving under my bed is forgotten altogether. I drink the tea, walk back to my bed and fall asleep immediately.

Six

It's the first day of my first grade. I'm terrified of being in school. I'm standing in the middle of the school yard and don't know where to go. I don't know who my teacher is. I don't know what to do. I have *no* clue about anything.

I see a familiar face—a girl in fifth grade who lives in our neighbourhood. I run to her and ask, "Please, could you take me home?"

The fifth grader laughs (at me, I think, but I can't worry about that right now) and says, "Go to the office, and find out where your class is."

I walk in the direction she shows me. I enter my class. My teacher is an elderly woman who gives me a dirty look for being late. I ignore her sour glance and walk all the way to the back of the classroom. I have found a good hiding place.

~~~

It's Thursday and the last hour of the school day. I'm being punished for not bringing my homework to school.

My teacher yells, "Go there and stand on one leg, next to the door, facing everyone, until the bell goes off!"

I walk to the door and stand on one leg, with my head down. Once or twice, I lift my head and look out at the school yard. My gaze goes through the square-shaped window in the middle of the door.

My sister is supposed to come soon and pick me up!

I worry, "I hope the teacher releases me from my punishment before my sister gets here."

I stand there for another hour, on one leg, and hear my classmates talking to each other. I think, "Good. They all are busy talking to each other. No one is noticing that I'm standing here, being punished. I can't see them, and they can't see me. Thank God, they can't see that I'm standing on one leg."

The bell goes off, and I run to the back of the classroom, grab my bag and run out very fast, thinking, "Nothing has happened. Nobody has noticed anything. I don't need to be embarrassed."

Without making eye contact with a single classmate, I run out, as if nothing has happened.

One Friday Afternoon

From the window of our living room, I see a white horse wandering on the grass field outside our house. The horse is limping, and it looks like one of his legs is broken! I call my brother, and together, we go to our father.

We ask him, "Dad, could we have this horse? Please, Please, Please!"

Dad answers, "If we had a bigger front yard, I would build a stable for him, and we would take care of him. Unfortunately, we don't, so we can't have him.

I think, "Such a shame! I like this white horse a lot!"

Too Quiet

I'm at our neighbour's house, painting with my friends. My friend's father is there too. He touches my thighs as we paint, sitting around a round table. I'm not comfortable, but I say nothing. He pulls his hand away when he sees one of his daughters is looking.

I don't like it here.

It seems that when you don't object to something that's wrong, some people just pretend that it is raining.

After a Few Months

The neighbour guy sees me in the common playground outside our home. He comes forward and asks, "Why aren't you coming to our house anymore? Come and play with the girls sometimes."

I answer, "Ok!"

I think, "Maybe he is realising what he was doing was wrong."

The Witch

Right in front of everyone, in the common play area outside our villa, my older sister hits me on the head, and says, "Oh, shut up, you witch!"

I feel numb and dizzy at the same time. Everyone is standing there—all my friends, the neighbour lady and her daughter with the handicap. There are other ladies too. Everyone sees what's happening. I just get hit in the head for no reason at all.

The 'lady teacher' in our neighbourhood yells, "Stop it! Why are you doing this?"

My sister rolls her eyes and leaves the scene.

I'm tearful. Still holding my head and wiping my tears, I walk toward the nice 'lady teacher' who defended me.

She asks me, "Are you okay, darling?"

I nod, still sobbing. I ask her, "I want to know what 'witch' means. Why is she calling me that?"

She looks like she's feeling sorry for me and doesn't want to say anything, but, reluctantly, she explains, "It means an ugly and deceitful creature!"

I feel sad to hear this, but safe knowing someone is standing up for me. I dare to ask again, "Why is she calling me this? I've never done anything to her, but she always seems to hate me."

The 'lady teacher' caresses my head at the spot where I got hit. She looks at me kindly and says, "She didn't mean anything, darling! Don't be upset!"

She gathers her children and walks toward their home which is only a few meters away from where we live.

Everyone knows the 'lady teacher' in our neighbourhood. She is educated and has read a million books. She doesn't mix with other ladies in the neighbourhood. While everyone else's hobby is to gather to cook and gossip, she keeps to herself.

Her favourite thing to say is, "Books are your best friends. At home, I travel everywhere through my books."

I love to read *Pippi Longstocking*. I absolutely adore this book. I love reading all about Tommy, Annika and the cookie jar from that store.

Often, we play 'make believe' with my friends. One of us is chosen to be Pippi, and the others are busy laughing and fixing her hair and putting dots on her cheeks to make her look like Pippi with all her freckles.

We weave one girl's hair like Pippi's, but it isn't standing up on the side like Pippi's hair, so we pick some broken branches from the ground to hold her hair up, dividing it into two parts.

"Oh my God, you look so funny! You look exactly like Pippi. She really looks like Pippi."

We all laugh loudly, while still fiddling with her hair, trying to hold the braids nicely up on the sides.

I love everything about Pippi's story.

Seven

It's summer, and I'm staying with my aunt. She lives in the middle of a forest, in a farmhouse made of wood. There is no electricity, so they cook food on burned wood. I love being here. I like this village and its simple life.

Every day, my cousins start a fire with logs to cook food on it. I love watching the fire, and I absolutely adore the smell of the burned wood on humid summer nights. I want to breathe in the smell of the burning wood, and I don't want to breathe it out.

I want this to be my experience forever and ever. I feel one with this feeling of the smell of the burned wood. Somehow, I disappear in it all. It takes me with itself to somewhere, and I don't even know where that somewhere is. I don't mind dying in this very moment with this feeling.

In the morning, for breakfast, I eat rice and sugar. It's so delicious. I'm not used to this kind of breakfast, but I still love it. My aunt is very nice. My cousins are very nice to me.

One Afternoon

It's hot. The sun is still shining fiercely. I'm walking around my aunt's house, up and down, barefoot, holding a broken branch in my hand. My two cousins and I are chatting and giggling at everything and nothing. I am happy being with them.

Suddenly, I see a thirty centimetre (or so) red snake. I jump, frightened! Then, we chase the poor snake and kill it, cutting it in two with a shovel. Even though it is sliced in half, the poor snake is still moving. We laugh our heads off and chase it further, smashing it so it is no longer moving. We bury it, laughing all the while.

We seem to be having lots of fun together.

One of Those Nights

My uncle is very upset with one of my older cousins. He wants to beat him up. He has been unruly! I'm very scared. I stand under the stairs, outside the door to the room where my uncle has locked himself and my cousin, so he can beat him up in peace. My other cousins don't look worried at all. In fact, they are all laughing. I hear screaming from inside the room.

My uncle screams, "Will you be listening from now on?"

My cousin screams louder and louder because he's getting beaten right and left with my uncle's belt.

Nobody dares to interfere. No one goes in to help him. I'm still the only one who looks very worried that my uncle might kill my cousin.

After ten minutes, my uncle comes out, followed by my cousin who smiles at me. I think,

"Thank God, he is alive!"

I still love my aunt's house made of wood, in the middle of this village. It's a true paradise.

Every night, we sleep under a net. It is my favourite time of the whole day. I love to listen to the barking of their dog, the sounds of the crickets, and all the other sounds that break the beautiful silence of the deep, dark nights.

We are on the second floor of their wooden house. I lay on the mattress spread out on the wooden floor, together with all my cousins. I look through the net encircling the whole sleeping area, not really noticing anyone around me, but feeling an indescribably good feeling.

Everywhere, it is quiet. We suddenly hear the dog barking. I guess someone is passing by the house.

In the heart of the pitch-black night with the singing of the crickets, I see a very dim light move, and I hear a soundless voice saying, "With you!"

My cousin, stretching his neck up, whispers, "The neighbour is coming home so late tonight!"

I sit up and lift the white, silky fly net, and, through the darkness, I see people walking behind the tall trees that are helping to create privacy. I smile. I am happy...

Three Weeks Later

I'm back in the city, back home. I love being home too. As soon as I enter the house, I hear my mom calling my name, "Come on, darling Rebecca! I made rice pudding for you! Do you want to scrape off the burned bottom that you love so much? I burned it extra, just the way you like it."

Happy Girl

I feel jolly today. I pick flowers from our garden and put them in vases all over the house. I dance, and I sing. Mother says, "These flowers aren't going to help with anything. Nothing can bring back his left eye. Things won't get pretty for us because of these flowers, sweetie…"

I stop arranging the flowers and sit on the couch next to mom.

"She is right. Things are awful. Flowers aren't going to help!"

Sadness

We are sitting in the kitchen, mom and I. She pours tea for me. She looks like she's been crying all night. It seems like she almost forced herself up to make breakfast for us before school. She looks *very* sad, and I feel very sad to see her sad.

I wish for my mom to be happy. She continues to cry silently, and I look at her through my downcast eyes. I can't drink my tea, as I feel a big lump in my throat.

She says, "Dad is always upset and angry with everything! He is always unhappy with anything I do. Nothing seems to make him really happy since we left behind the left eye of your brother at the hospital."

Banana

Some days, dad is ok. Like today. He is coming out of his car in our front yard. He is holding a bag full of bananas. We see him holding the bag, and we squeal with joy. It seems we like bananas. Dad's very happy to see us happy.

Nine

I stand outside the classroom with my mom and my fourth grade teacher. My mother is talking to my teacher about my non-progress in school. Suddenly, mom slaps me in front of my teacher and all of my classmates.

I freeze! I hope, with all my heart, "No one saw what happened, no one saw what happened…"

My teacher—I think she looks happy—asks me to get back to the classroom. I go back to my bench, put my head on the table and hope no one has noticed.

I hear one of my classmates whispering to another, "Why did her mom do that? Why did she do it here? Why didn't she wait to get home first and then deal with her?"

I hide my face more on my hugged elbows, and think, somewhat desperately, "I wish that I could just melt away into thin air! I don't want to feel anything."

My teacher is back in the classroom, already engaged in a deep discussion with the class about the element of choice in one's life, completely indifferent to how I am.

She says, "Listen everyone! What if someone tells you that you've chosen *everything* that has ever happened to you in your life until today? Let's think about it for a moment and discuss this in detail!"

I frown, my head still resting on the school desk, shamefully, over my crossed arms.

I am angry. I think, "What choice? What the hell is she talking about? How could I have chosen my horrible mother? How could I have chosen my insensitive teacher? How could I have chosen what's happening to me now? How can anyone choose the endurance of this pain and loneliness? How could anyone want to be so totally ashamed and feel as small as I feel right at this moment? How?"

My eyes burn with anger and tears start to roll, and as I hold the left side of my face, I just wish that the pain I'm feeling would subside.

That Afternoon

I go home. I see my mom in the garden. She is watering the plants. The hose is in her hand as I pass her by to head inside the house. She looks at me, with seeming indifference, yet, saying to me with her eyes, "It isn't a big deal! Mothers hit their children and children forget all about it. Get over it!"

She continues to water the flowers as if nothing happened. I don't say anything.

Late in the Evening

I sit by my desk, trying to do my school work. My dad calls me from a distance. I run fast to him to see what he wants. He is standing with a friend, by the stairs, right before entering the front yard. He asks, "Where are those VCR tapes I told you to keep for my friend?"

I answer, with a big smile on my face, "Oh, I loaned them to a friend. She will give them back to me next week."

"Why the hell did you do that? I told you to keep them at home. There is a reason why I said that. Why don't you understand? Why don't you ever listen?"

His voice gets louder and harsher with each sentence he throws at me.

I freeze at this verbal attack, that too in front of my dad's friend. All I can do is to hang my head, as if in remorse. Dad's friend yells gently, "Stop it!"

Dad stops.

I stand there a few more seconds. I do not know what to do, since both dad and his friend are pretending that I'm not there anymore. I drag myself quietly toward the living room, then run inside to my room, behind the desk, trying to pull myself together so I can continue with my school work. My face is still flushed, and my focus is gone.

My head is a tumble of thoughts.

"What just happened? Did he hit me, too? No, that was in the morning. Mom hit me this morning in school, and now, dad was just yelling at me. It was nothing. This was nothing. It's not a big deal."

My thoughts drift, "Is it possible? That we've chosen everything? Even our parents? Let me try this in writing as the teacher asked us to do in class.

Almost as if on its own, my pen starts writing. It is as if my thoughts and my pen have become one.

It is once upon a time. I am here, and, at the same time, I am not here. I am in a place that isn't a place I know at all. I can't see anyone or anything, but I am everywhere, and yet, nowhere.

I try to *feel* what I'm feeling in this Once Upon A Time, "Oh, so interesting! What is it that I'm feeling here? It feels and smells so familiar, and so fresh. I want to run toward this familiar freshness with this familiar smell. I'm loving this familiarity. I want this smell. I want to melt into it. I know this with all my being! I want this."

I just know that I have to go down this path. I want to sit here and just be here forever.

I keep moving through this nowhere-everywhere place, without moving a muscle.

~~~

I see a café.

A twenty-seven-year-old guy with a black scarf around his neck sits at one end, all alone, drinking by himself, quietly observing his surroundings.

Two giggling girls in their mid-twenties—seemingly sisters—walk toward the café, with many bags in their hands, debating whether they should sit and have a cup of tea or not.

The younger girl with longer hair notices—at once—the serious guy with the black scarf around his neck, sipping his tea.

Their eyes meet, and they smile at each other. The younger girl with long hair says, "Yes! We *should* sit here in this café and have something to drink."

They sit down, intentionally, near the serious-looking guy with the black scarf.

The scene shifts.

I now see them getting married.

Now I see them with my two sisters.

And now I see myself, making the choice to go to this setting…

It smells and feels good—drifting to this setting…

~~~~

I am finished with my writing, still smiling. The slap from my mother in front of all my classmates and my father's yelling weren't hurting anymore. It seems that when I was busy writing, I forgot everything else.

In a voice I haven't heard before, spoken by someone I cannot see, I hear,

"You've arranged this whole thing! You chose them, and, at the same time, they called for you. You chose them, and they chose you. They smelled and looked familiar to you. Everything about them was pleasantly familiar for you. All you had to do was just drift toward them.

You went that way because that was the only way you could go, and yet, you went toward them willingly and by choice. Only it was a choice-less choice. This happened. You choose that direction because you liked that smell and the feeling of it. You were drawn to it without knowing the why and the how. It just happened."

I hear my mom calling me to go and have dinner. I continue to hear that soundless voice while walking,

"Are you where you want to be? Maybe not! But, for sure, you are where you ought to be!"

~~~~

No one talks to one another. Dinner time passes quietly. I'm actually happy that no one is talking.

After dinner, I go straight to bed, trying to read some pages of my favourite book, *Desire*. Desire's story keeps me awake way past midnight.

Full House

We always have friends over. Mom makes food for us, and we stay in our room and hang around with our friends. Mom and dad don't seem to mind this at all. Dad always says that he prefers having our friends in our home, rather than letting us go to them.

"I know who *I* am, I don't know who they are," he says.

Walk in the Park

The government is overthrown, and everyone is rushing to the park to see the biggest news at this moment. Dead bodies hang from trees everywhere! I try not to look as my mother and I walk through the park.

Mom says, "Good! These bastards have been torturing people for years and years, they deserve what they've got."

I'm terrified. I see a hand, which has been cut from someone's body, hanging from one tree. I see another body hanging by its feet on another tree, with its intestines hanging out from its slashed stomach.

I look at mom, trying to avoid looking at the trees. We walk into a very dark area, and I hear people whispering, "*This* was their human-burning dungeon!"

We walk back home, quietly.

This was the same park dad always brought us to play in. Today, it wasn't quite the same.

Weak Girl

I hear my mom and dad talking about me, "Rebecca is weak in her studies. She can't concentrate well. She isn't like the other two girls."

They don't know that I can hear them. They are right—I am slow. And I am the weakest at home.

Movie Time

All of us are sitting in the living room and watching movies. We all seem happy! We like to watch movies together. Whenever we are home, this is what we do—eat and watch movies...

Eleven

I'm eleven. I write on a piece of paper, "I wish I could see my friends again!"

I see my sister getting ready to go out, and I try to put the note on the ground because I know she will be passing by. I want her to read it and feel sorry for me. I actually also want her to give me permission, so I can go and see my friends. I seem to need her permission. She goes out, walking over my begging note. She doesn't see it. I'm left alone with my frustration. I want to see my friends, but I can't, and I'm not happy.

I seem to be okay to let others do whatever they like, and my response, every time, is the same.

Nothing!

I let others do whatever they want with me.

I'm very good at this...

The Spinster Teacher

I'm in the Arabic classroom, in my first year of middle school. I like this teacher. She is somehow different. She looks like a man with a ponytail, with a hairy face. She is not married, so I guess she isn't allowed to remove the hair growing on her face. Facial hair or not, she is kind.

She is different from other teachers and calls us by our first names. She says, "Each person is unique. Each one deserves to be respected and be called by their own name!"

It feels strange when she calls me by my first name, but I feel comfortable in her classroom.

Sweet Dad

My dad is very sweet with others, but he has a sour and edgy attitude as soon as he gets home. It's almost like he has a double personality. It is very hard to believe when everyone says that he is famous for being the coolest guy ever among his friends and co-workers!

Angry Dad

Dad is hitting my brother because he is clumsy. My mom is nervous. I feel worried and sad. My brothers are naughty.

Dad is always upset, always rushing us. We are always being rushed in stores, even in parties! We are always hurrying to do something. I feel I'm always in a hurry. I'm always worried when I'm with my family.

The Pirogue Guy

The school bell goes off. I hurry to get out of the classroom, eager to get out of school. He stands there, outside of school, dark-skinned, tall and bold. He has a big, silver-coloured tray on top of his head with lots of sweet pirogues—sugary, delicious donuts—on it.

He is chanting, "These are pirogues! They are from Tehran!"

He continues repeating these chants over and over again. A wide smile on my face, I am eager to reach him before anyone else. I buy two pirogues, and I take a bite immediately. I love the juicy, creamy custard inside. I love the spongy texture when I bite into the round, plump pirogues.

I walk home, smiling, skipping and happy. I am in seventh heaven with the other pirogue in my hand.

No Encouragement

I look enthusiastic as I hear the front gate opening and dad's car pulling in. I run to the front yard. Dad doesn't look happy, but I'm eager to tell him something.

"Dad! You know what? There are these cassettes and a book. I can learn English in my sleep by just listening to the tape throughout the night while sleeping. Please, please, can I buy it?"

Dad looks indifferent to my eagerness, takes out some money from his pocket, hands it to me and says, "Here, take this money and go and buy it. I want to see what the hell you are going to do!"

The money is in my hand, and dad goes upstairs. I stand there, trying to digest what I have just heard. Relieved that no one else is around, I go inside. I am suddenly not sure if I want to buy this tape anymore.

Two Days Later

I try the tape, but I'm bothered. I don't want to do it, yet I keep thinking, "Dad didn't mean to be mean! He probably wanted to encourage me!"

Twelve

I vomit all over the floor. My mom cleans the floor, and dad stands there, watching me, looking concerned. Dad is concerned. He is kind.

Engagement Party

It is one of my older cousins' engagement party. The party seems like a wedding with music, dinner, cake and hundreds of guests on the list.

Everything is prepared. My mom is one of the organisers and seems very busy.

The usually muddy yard of my favourite auntie's wooden home is all sanded so that the guests can easily walk without getting wet and messy.

Lights of different colours are arranged neatly on trees and it is giving this wooden house, in the middle of thousands of trees and an ocean of rice fields, a divine appearance.

I stand on the second floor, in the all-around-open veranda that I know so well from all those summer nights I spent there. Memories of those nights under the fly net come rushing back as I observe everyone being busy, adding the final touches before the guests arrive.

Seeing the drizzle of rain and smelling the wet wood again feels like being in paradise. I walk down the wooden stairs to the first floor and then through the open veranda downstairs, toward the second set of stairs that lead to the big yard.

I think, "I love this place and everything about it. The feeling of wood underneath my feet when I walk down the stairs, the smell of wet wood, the smell of wet trees, the smell of the burned wood. I love these roosters singing and the dogs barking. I can imagine living here forever."

The party starts and everyone is dancing. It's a very happy party.

Late at Night

By now, all the guests are gone, and all the cousins from different uncles and aunties are put in one room to sleep. I, too, am inside that room.

It is past midnight, and I wake up because I feel something odd. It feels too hot. It is difficult to breathe—someone is very tightly close to my back. I push the person away and say, "Why are you so tightly close to me? Please give me some room, it's not comfortable like this!"

I try to go back to sleep. A few minutes pass, and again I feel something rubbing against my lower spine. I sit up without looking back and without saying anything.

I move to keep good distance from the person who was behind me, but, for the rest of the hours until morning, I'm not able to sleep. Thinking, "I need to be awake. I have to be awake. I feel safer if I'm awake."

Six O'Clock in the Morning

I hear mom talking to my aunty! I hurry out of the room, stand beside them, and think, "Should I say something to mom?"

Mom is busy talking to aunty, barely noticing me standing there, looking all pale and upset.

We are leaving for home. I have to change my uniform, and then I have to head to school as soon as possible.

In the taxi, I think, "Maybe I imagined what happened last night…"

I can't breathe. I want to scream, but I can't scream. I feel a lump in my throat. I want to cry but can't. I want to talk to someone, but I feel I can't.

I choose to be silent.

I find myself standing in the school yard, wearing my light grey school uniform. It is a full-length dress, very formless, tasteless and of a very sad colour.

Now I am right in front of my classroom. When did I get here? I hear the bell, but I'm still frozen. I can't move. I'm still. To a blank point.

I think, "What might be the colour of the despair that I'm feeling right at this moment? As depressing as the colour of my school uniform? What is the colour of the volcano of tears that isn't coming out from my eyes?"

I am feeling numb and still wondering, "Did it really happen? Or did I dream about it all? What happened? Am I dreaming now?"

I *need* to talk. I need to tell. I should tell mom that I have already had my period several times. I need to start speaking. I feel like I'm choking. I can't breathe. I want to breathe, and I *need* to talk.

My eyes wander around in the school yard. I look for my Arabic teacher. I can't see her. With tears in my eyes and a heaviness in my shoulders, I think, "If I see her right at this moment, I swear I will tell her everything!"

Kind Dad

I sit on a boat with my whole family, on a ride on the lake in the dam covered with a million lotus flowers. It seems that it's one of those days, perhaps it is the effect of this paradise-like nature. I look like I'm sitting there, but I'm actually in another world. I am forced to come out of my flawless thoughtlessness, though, when I hear the boat driver tell my dad, "Their report cards are out, I have heard. So tell me, which one of these five should be thrown into this lake?"

I just remember that I, in fact, have several not-very-good marks on my card. At that moment, my eyes meet my dad's eyes. He's smiling at me, and, at the same time, at his comment, or so it seems. He says, "No! Everyone has done excellent!"

Violent Dad

We visit my aunt—my dad's sister. My aunt's home is a twenty-minute drive from our home.

My sister and I are in the car, on our way back home. My uncle is driving. I'm ringing the bell non-stop: ding ding, ding ding. I am, seemingly, in a childish mood. My sister is standing by the door eagerly so that she can rush in as soon as the door is open. I still press the bell happily. Dad opens the door. He looks mad, his eyes burning with anger. He grabs my sister by the hair. I pull back, hearing my uncle from behind.

Uncle screams, "Let go! Let go of her! What the hell are you doing?"

Dad lets go of her, and we all go inside.

Normal

The volume on the television is high, and dad shouts his head off over this, "Why the hell is the TV so loud? Switch the damn thing off. Why the hell do you have the volume so loud?"

He screams literally from the bottom of his lungs. His eyes are red, and he smells of alcohol.

I fearfully answer, "I'm sorry. I will turn it down!"

I'm afraid that he will jump and grab me by the neck any second. I'm scared all the time. When he is angry, I feel he can kill someone easily. Even when he is not around, I hear and fear him.

I am always worried about dad's sour mood, even before he comes home. I am worried when he is hungry, when he is upset with us, when he is upset with life, when he is upset with mom. I am *always* worried about dad's moods.

I constantly worry about what's going to happen next. I feel that I should do *something* to prevent and fix the damage before it gets totally out of hand.

I feel I have to be awake all the time, have to be ready at all times, in case dad is in one of his bad moods.

Disturbed

My two brothers are being chased by dad. He wants to grab them so he can beat them up. Why? Because the door of the bedroom is slammed by the draught in the house and because he suddenly wakes up from his afternoon nap. Then, of course, *someone* has to be punished for that.

My brothers are fast enough, and dad can't catch up at first. He is beating those unfortunate little boys with his favourite belt. Dad's voice changes into a mix of a barking and wounded dog.

I fear the sound of his voice. There is a feeling of fear in our surroundings, possibly even in the very walls of our house.

Dad never seems to need to chase, grab or hit me because I know how to be good. I know how to be quiet. I know how not to stir things up.

I know very well how to never make anyone upset. But I hear his screaming voice even when he is not around.

Thirteen

In our living room, I am scared and shaking. My dad is yelling at my mom, and my mom is cursing my aunts—my dad's sisters, of course.

I'm in-between them, trying to prevent a possible physical attack. While holding dad's mouth, so he stops shouting, I'm crying and begging them to stop, terrified that the argument *will* escalate further.

No one is there, but mom, dad and I. I wonder, "Where are my brothers and sisters? Why am I the only one in the middle of this war zone?"

I try to stop it all by myself.

Sister's Sour Look

We are all on a family picnic on the mountain near our city. I'm so hungry, I grab a sandwich to eat. My sister gives me a dark, sour look and says, "Why the hell did you take that? I was going to have it."

I say, "Come, take it! Looks like you need it more."

I see the grinding teeth of my sister, I guess she doesn't like my sarcastic remark. I wish I wasn't taking that bite at all...

Next-Door Neighbour

Our next-door neighbour is a widow. Everyone thinks she is crazy. She is also called the area's 'nosy officer' because her nose is in everybody's business! She has a twenty-year-old handicapped daughter.

I'm over at her place to just sit with her daughter until the mom comes back. The girl can't talk, walk or do anything by herself. I'm doing my homework over there. After an hour, her mom's back. She sees me doing my homework and says, "Why are you writing like this? Do use a different colour pen. Look! You aren't doing it beautifully. Is this your friend's handbook? Look! She writes so nicely. Why don't you do it like her?"

My head is down, and I say nothing.

The Good Girl

Dad calls me, "Bring me a glass of water! I need to take my medicine!"

He has a severe cold. Everyone is running around, getting ready for our spring holiday.

Dad says, in an annoyed tone, "I have to get rid of this damn cold, so I can drive for nine hours today."

I'm very happy about our upcoming holiday. I walk to the kitchen, get tap water in a glass and hand it to him.

I sit in front of him, with a big smile on my face. He takes a sip and, right away, spits it straight into my face.

He looks very angry and says, "This bloody water is not cold enough! You know that I like cold water!"

Stunned and speechless, with my head down, wiping the mixture of water, medicine and dad's saliva off my face, I stand up quietly and just walk away.

It seems like I know how to do this. I know how to not complain and how to not object.

I know how to say nothing.

I know how to be quiet, and I know how to let people do whatever pleases them.

Friend's Home

I am on the way to my friend's home. We are supposed to study English together.

Her father is home. I'm not comfortable. He comes into the room while we are studying. He stands next to me and looks at our notes. Before he leaves the room, he strokes himself against my leg. I pretend that I don't notice.

I am good at pretending that everything is ok, even when most things aren't.

My 13th Birthday

It is the morning of my birthday. I'm awake and all excited. I'm looking for the phone to ring my friends.

I enter the living room and see mom sitting on the floor, bending over, with a screwdriver in her hand. The green telephone is shattered to pieces, and she is trying to put it together.

Mom doesn't lift her head. She's crying, "Don't worry, it's almost fixed!"

I ask, "Dad?"

"*Yes!*"

"Why is the sewing machine on the floor?"

She looks at me.

I realise!

Poor mom, trying to fix the phone! She is good at fixing. She is good at covering things up.

Quiet Girl

I'm fourteen, and my body is changing, and I don't like it at all. I'm not walking proudly. I'm wearing baggy clothes all the time. I don't want my breasts to show. I don't like my new body at all. I feel ugly.

~~~~

I'm in my friend's house. Her father is explaining how to measure the square meters of a room to my friend.

I'm very surprised to see him, as I thought it would be only my friend and me. She walks to the other room with the measuring tape.

I say, "I'll come back later!"

She yells, "No, wait! I'm done in a couple of minutes!"

I am standing next to him and feeling extremely awkward. He puts his hand through my blouse and touches my breast. My face turns red! I frown and want to say something, anything that will stop him, but I just stand there, and I let him.

I don't know how to say "No." I haven't learned this.

He takes some coins out of his pocket and hands them to me, while he is instructing my friend how to do the measuring. I shake my head, refusing to take the money. My friend comes back, and he hurriedly takes his hand off me.

I tell my friend that I have to go, and I leave immediately. I'm not screaming. I want to tell someone, but I'm not telling anyone. I run toward home, feeling dirty. I want to tell mom.

Then I remember my dad and the VCR tapes and the spitting. I remember my mom and the slapping.

I reach home. I go to my room. I don't feel like telling anybody! I hate my body.

The Letter

An argument is going on between my mom and dad. It's about my aunts. Mom loves talking about my aunt's dirty laundry. Mom is disappointed again.

Dad is quiet right now. He looks like he will be throwing back words to her at any time.

~~~~

It is in the middle of one summer day. Dad's cousin, the childless one, is dead.

At his memorial service, the ladies are gathered together. They are busy talking about my mom. The widow of the deceased cousin is cursing my mom loudly, "I wish you all the pain and misery in life!"

She speaks as if my mom is the one who killed her husband.

In Our Home

Mom isn't sad at all about the departure of the childless cousin. She is being notified about what went on at the funeral. She smiles at what she hears, at first, but suddenly she feels the pinch. She feels she has to give them the answer they deserve in a letter.

Mom writes about all their dirty laundry throughout their lives, their pre and post-marital scandals, etc.

Her three-page letter finishes like this,

"First and foremost, please go through your own history before unfairly mentioning my name anywhere else!"

Yes! My mother likes to answer back, and she likes to write letters.

That Night

It is past midnight, during the early hours of a Wednesday, and a very loud screaming sound wakes me up!

"What's happening? War? Bomb? Attack? Dying? What?"

My whole body trembles uncontrollably. I don't know what's happening. Halfway between sitting and standing up from my bed, my legs begin shaking so violently that I have to hold them with my equally trembling hands.

I hear screaming, "I wish to God that you die! You bloody, miserable woman! Come out you bloody whore! I will rip you apart with my own hands. Because of your stupid letter, my husband has thrown me out of the house, and now, my brother must throw you out of this house."

It's my aunt who is screaming from outside, right in the middle of the street. I'm still shaking. I hear the crowds of neighbours outside our front door.

I think, "Oh my God! Everyone is hearing all this! Oh my God! We won't be able to raise our heads in this neighbourhood anymore."

My father walks outside. He speaks softly, trying to calm his sister down. This is the first time I hear my dad speak softly.

My aunt is still shouting, "You are not a real man! Throw this whore out of your house! Bring that whore wife of yours out here, so I can rip her big stupid mouth apart, so I can break her fingers one by one, so she never can write a letter like this again!"

I think, "It's not only us, but all the neighbours in the compound can hear her too. I guess even the Mayor of the city is awake by now and can hear her. I hope he sends the police soon."

I hear my dad—in the saddest tone of voice—say, "Look, everyone! See! This is my sister who is shouting like this!"

I am still standing by the staircase before our front yard with my two younger brothers, who are also listening fearfully, like me, to this drama.

I hear the police siren, and I see the red and blue shifting lights. The front door opens, dad comes in and closes the door quickly behind him. He says, "I'm going to change so I can go to the police station."

He mumbles, while throwing a sad and sour look at mom, standing by the door of our living room.

He says to mother, while passing her by, "You need to change and come too!"

Dad is very short in his wording. He has no power to say more. He isn't his normal shouting self, right at this moment.

My aunt is suddenly quiet, but her husband who has just arrived in another car takes over and starts shouting and banging and kicking on our front door which is made of iron.

I worry, "Can he break the iron door? What will happen if he manages to get in?"

He yells, "Where are they? Where is she? Open this damn door. Come on out. Why aren't you opening the door?"

I'm so frightened that I jump and switch the light off.

My aunt's husband continues shouting, "Why are you switching off the light? Hey, everyone, it is the house of '…' " He keeps yelling our last name!

The policeman is trying to calm him down, and, by now, mom and dad are walking out to follow them to the station.

I try to go back to sleep, my body still trembling. I can't sleep. I don't want to sleep. I have to be awake, in case… I hope that mom and dad will be back safely. I fall asleep eventually.

The Next Morning

As soon as I wake up, I hear mom and dad's voices. I try to get up. I can't stand up. My left knee is totally locked. I try to stretch my knee, but it's not possible.

I shout, "Mom! I can't move. My left knee is locked!"

Psychological

I have been taken to a doctor, and the conclusion is that nothing is wrong with me physically. That my knee is getting locked every now and then, is ONLY psychological.

Understanding

It hurts when I pee. I tell my mom, and mom looks concerned. At the table, when eating lunch, mom tells my dad that she has to take me to see a doctor.

Dad asks, "What for?"

My mom looks at me, and then she answers, "None of your business!"

It sounds funny—my mom telling my dad off and trying to sound like she is joking. I feel good somehow because I feel she doesn't want to embarrass me by talking to my dad about my painful peeing.

Mean Girl

We have a full house. My elder sister's in-laws are staying with us for a week. We are happy to have visitors, but we are very busy. I see that I'm not nice to my little brother. I speak to him like an unkind older sister. I correct him and boss him around in front of our guests. It seems I feel good doing this. My little brother doesn't say anything.

I have learned to be mean.

Tolerant Girl

My older sister is moving to another country to join her husband. He has already been living there for the last two years. My sister goes out every day with her friends to buy all that she needs for her move.

Today, I'm out with my sister and her friends. I'm in pain. I have my painful period. I have cramps. On and off, I feel cold sweat, yet I continue to walk around with them. It's in the middle of July, a very hot and humid day. I think, "I should have stayed at home and rested. I should just turn around and go home. I shouldn't have come out with them at all."

I hope that someone notices that I'm in pain and tells me that I can go home. No one talks to me. Nobody even notices that I'm here and in pain and drenched in cold sweat. Nobody wants me there.

"Soon it will be finished. Soon we'll go home."

I feel so thirsty, hungry, dizzy on this hot July day, and I don't ask to stop and buy something to drink.

I don't know how to ask for help, and they are good at not offering. An hour has passed, we are still walking around. I listen to their conversation and look at all the things they are buying. Finally, we are on our way home.

"Oh, home, sweet home!"

Never has it been lovelier to reach home. I walk straight to our living room and lie down on one of the couches.

"Oh God! I'm so tired. I want to die. I have so much pain in my tummy. I wish I just didn't wake up anymore."

That Evening

I am awake and alive! It's seven o'clock. I've been sleeping for four hours straight! It's still very hot, and there is no AC in our bedroom. I'm sharing a bedroom with my other sister who is one year older than I am.

We have fun with our little broken fan in our room. We are laughing about the non-functioning swing action of our fan. The fan is in-between our beds, with two strings hanging on each side of it.

I laugh, pulling the string toward me so that the fan blows air on me!

My sister, Tara, does the same. We giggle about our fan with its home-made, manual swing action—the latest model indeed!

After One Year

It's time to go! The car is packed, and I hug and kiss everyone for the last time. I'm leaving the house I grew up in. It's not a big deal that I'm leaving my home and my country. I don't seem to feel bothered at all.

A neighbouring friend comes to visit me to say goodbye to me and my mom. She whispers with a smile, "Say a real good goodbye to her," and she points to my grandma who is over eighty. "For sure, you won't see her anymore!"

I smile back and recall asking my grandma once, "Grandma! How old are you?"

She had responded, "None of your business!"

Without any dramatic and tearful ceremony, I get into the car to leave my hometown forever, not knowing that the very first chapter of my life has come to an end right here, right at this moment.

Moved

I enter the second part of my life...

Copenhagen

Landing in the airport with my mom and from behind all—passport controls, thick glass, too many people—I see my sister and her husband waving happily. I run fast toward the thick glass where my sister is standing, and I kiss the glass. I can't understand why I'm pretending like this. I'm happy to be here and see her, but I feel this kissing-the-glass-thing is only a pretence.

Home

And without any effort at all, I feel right at home here.

This makes me wonder, "Did I leave home? Or did I just get home?"

Snow

How can one write enough about the beauty of snow? Everywhere I look, the ground is covered with snow.

It is winter 1987, and Scandinavia is hit by the snowiest winter of all time. I feel like I am in the middle of a snowy paradise.

I am living with my sister and her husband. They are helping me with the steps necessary to be able to stay here.

Mother Leaves

One month has gone by. We drop my mom at the airport and are buying groceries before going home. I stand beside my sister, waiting for the meat slices to be cut and ready, and I feel this chunk of sadness in my throat. I want to run away, and I want to cry, but I hold it all in.

I miss my mom already.

New Life

I go to my language school every day for a couple of hours, and then I go home. My sister and I then prepare the food, tidy and clean up, sometimes buy groceries or go for a run in the neighbourhood.

Overall, it's different to live here. While I like being in Denmark, I feel like I'm under constant supervision which I'm not used to at all. My brother-in-law likes to find fault in everything that I do.

I don't have my own room. I sleep in the living room. Every night, I have to wait for everyone to be finished with watching television, and when they are done, I spread the mattress out and then go to sleep. Sometimes, I'm very sleepy and tired, and I don't like this waiting at all. I don't feel comfortable just laying down here while others are watching TV or there in the room.

During the day, it is much easier, as I'm at school, learning the Danish language.

Sweet Eighteen

My sister invites some of their friends for my eighteenth birthday. There is food to be cooked and cake to be made. I am sent several times to the store—which is five minutes walking distance from their home—to buy the currently missing ingredient.

When I'm on the way to the store for the third time, to buy the missing tomato paste, I'm frustrated and thinking, "I could easily live without this bothersome birthday party!"

Ice Cream and Coffee

I've made a friend in my language classes. Her name is Sari. I'm invited to her home. My sister says we should not let her husband know that I'm going to visit my friend.

I find this very strange as I don't understand. It is none of his business where I go and who I see.

I go to my friend, Sari, anyway, and her mom serves us coffee and ice cream.

I love this combination—something very cold with something very hot. I love it!

Clever Girl

Within a year, I speak the Danish language fluently. I feel good, and I'm ready to be on my own. My sister doesn't want me to move out but helps me find a place near their home anyway.

On My Own in Cumin Street Nr. 8

The saying has it, "There is a first time for everything in life!"

This is the first time I'm living by myself. I have a tiny little studio flat. I can walk across all of it in less than five seconds. Yet, it is my own.

My first night here feels strange. It's too quiet at first. Then, as I lie in bed, I hear a few guys outside. They are singing, talking, swearing and cheering.

It's the middle of winter, and every day and night, it is freezing outside, almost 20 degrees below zero. I like to leave the window next to my bed open, just a couple of centimetres, for the cool breeze freshens my tiny room. I love the fresh, snowy air cutting through the warmth of my little studio flat and touching my nostrils. It makes me feel alive.

Those drunken guys are right under my window on the street, and although my flat is four stories up, I can hear them clearly, as if they were with me inside the flat.

It's comforting to have them and hear them. I feel safe in their company.

I am still, lying in my bed, looking at the ceiling, breathing the freezing air, hearing the guys outside and listening to Dolly Parton singing on television, "And I... will always love you…"

My First Word of Encouragement

In front of my whole language class, my teacher, Vicky, announces, "Rebecca must be proud of herself, as she is the best student with the highest score in this class."

I am super happy. *Never* have I heard something like this, but before she calls out my name, somehow, I know I'm the best in this class already. Somehow, I know that I am very able.

Careful Girl

I enjoy my language classes. I laugh a lot with my classmates. It's fun to be around them because I get to be myself. No one finds fault in my every move.

Blagoy is my Yugoslavian classmate. He calls out to me one afternoon.

"Let's go for a drive and have a bite to eat!"

I say, "I don't want to!"

He is a nice guy, always happy and friendly, but I don't go out with him. I seem to be ok just being at home after school.

First Job

I have a job! It is in the kitchen of an elderly home nearby, just a five minutes' walk from my studio flat in Cumin street number 8. I love working here—washing dishes, making food and sandwiches. I like the people I work with, and they like working with me, although I am not close to anyone...

I don't have friends of my own.

Fixed Up

My sister's friend is fixing me up with the brother of another friend, and I agree to meet him. I seem very ok with others planning things for me. I think, "They are older than I, so they must know better. Others always know better!"

First Kiss on My Hand

On my way back—in the walking distance between work and home—I can feel someone following me. I look back, and I see this blond guy smiling at me. I continue walking. I'm by the front door of my building, and before I enter, he catches up and says, "I'm from Finland. How are you?"

I smile and say, "I live here!"

I stretch out my arm to shake hands. He takes my hand and kisses it.

I smile again and bound up to the fourth floor...

The Arranged Date

It's Saturday, and I'm in Copenhagen's oldest park, the Garden of Rosenborg Castle, for my 'date.' It feels awkward. We aren't talking. We walk around a little. He finally says, "Would you like to watch a movie?"

I agree, and we sit in his car and go to the cinema. I try to pay attention to the movie, but watching him is more interesting.

He laughs out loud, excitedly, while eating his popcorn. Both his feet are up and rested on the seats in the previous row. He looks as if he is at home, and no one else is with him. It's almost as if he doesn't know that I'm here either. He seems very comfortable with himself.

I think, "He is ok. I like him!"

Two Weeks Later

Just like that, it's my engagement party. I'm dressed in a flowery dress that my sister sewed for me. I arrange the table for dinner. My fiancé is entertaining his sister and nephew. He doesn't seem excited.

I don't feel excited. I'm ok with what's happening, but not in seventh heaven.

He is with me, but I feel he isn't with me. When we go out, he is verbal, and sometimes physical, with everyone almost all the time. When I speak, he contradicts me in front of others. I feel afraid of opening my mouth and saying anything when he is around. I don't like *anything* about him, but I'm ok with it. I'm pushing very hard for marriage.

The Night Before the Wedding

Fifty guests have already been invited, and the plan is for me to wear my sister's wedding dress. Don't they say it's not a good omen to wear someone else's wedding dress? But I'm excited about the wedding anyway. At least I get to be dressed in white and feel all special.

My sister seems excited too. I will be married, become a respectable woman and be someone else's responsibility from now on.

~~~~

It's seven in the evening, and I am over at my fiancé's place, arranging the next day's dinner with my sister. The bell rings. He opens the door. I hear his sister's voice. I think, "Great! Another pair of hands to help!"

She doesn't look happy, barely smiles when she says hello. She asks to speak to him alone. I am in the kitchen with my sister, and they walk to the next room. There is a wall in-between. She is whispering, but I still can hear her.

"Since you have been going out with her, you haven't been paying enough attention to me and my son. You need to think this over very carefully!"

While my sister-in-law-to-be is trying to break up my marriage, which is supposed to happen tomorrow, my sister and I are still in the kitchen, smirking and making fun of her stupid attempt. I'd be lying if I say I'm not worried.

He walks out with his sister. My sister is leaving too. I'm in bed, worried, thinking, "It doesn't look good!"

The Wedding Ceremony

Everyone is present here, waiting for the minister to start.

The minister asks, "Where are the parents of the beloved couple?"

A long, cold and deadening silence takes over the room. No one looks at anyone else. All heads are down. It looks almost like someone's death sentence is about to be read.

My sister breaks the silence, "Unfortunately, the parents couldn't get a visa, so they couldn't make it."

The minister looks at everyone and, smiling quickly, pretends that he hasn't been noticing the awkward energy surrounding this crowd.

The ceremony starts, and all the 'Yes's' and all the signatures are received in an uneasy quiet. No smiles, no fireworks and no flying money for a good omen!

It looks more like a funeral than a wedding. It's like somehow everyone knows that there is no love and happiness here, and yet, everyone, including and especially me, are ok with it in a very disturbed way.

I look nervous, and he still looks like he is in a bad mood. He says in a clearly annoyed tone, "I'll take you to the beauty salon!"

Beauty Salon

For two hours, the beauty specialist fixes my hair and face, while I lie to her on and off about how sad I am that my parents aren't here.

I pray for some magical power to make everything rosy and beautiful.

Photo Shoot

I am in the car now, on the way to a flower shop to pick my bridal bouquet and then heading toward the photographer to take our memorable first pictures as husband and wife.

He hasn't spoken to me at all the whole day, but now he says, again with a tone of annoyance, "Let's just do what the photographer says and get it over with, so we can get to the wedding hall!"

This whole thing feels like a tour of duty that's dragging and trying everyone's patience.

I smile, pretending that I don't notice his tone at all. I am good at this! "This is not happening at all. Nobody is noticing! Everything is good."

Wedding Party

We are in the basement, under his flat, just about to enter the hall. As soon as we enter a roomful of cheering guests, he lightens up, and his mood changes. He seems to be in a party mood now. I also relax and get busy mingling with all our friends. I'm happy that no scandal has occurred so far, and I'm still married.

The Next Morning

On our way to my studio flat with him. He is quiet again. It seems he still isn't sure about our marriage. I'm nervous again. We get into the flat without talking to each other. In less than an hour, the cleaning is done, and before we leave the flat, he looks defeated and says, "I can't do this! I don't want to be married to you. This is a mistake!"

I'm tearful, and my whole body begins to shake. He notices, and doesn't even bother to hide the half-smirking smile on his face. I read on his face, and in his eyes, "Why is she like that? Am I so good that she is shaking at the sheer thought of losing me?"

I cry, "No! Don't say this! You are tired after the wedding and all. You will feel different soon. Don't be like this!"

He insists, "No! This won't work. You should continue staying in your flat."

I threaten, "If you do this, I will drink this Clorox!"

Stunned by what he's seeing, he stares at me for a couple of seconds and then just walks toward the door, saying, "See you at home! We will talk about it later."

I feel ashamed but victorious. I can stay married, and no one else needs to know about this.

Six Months Later—Earthquake

It's summer, and I've booked a ticket to travel home and see my parents for a month.

An 8.7 magnitude earthquake on the Richter scale has hit the north of Iran. I weep because I think all my family are dead. The pictures on the news are absolutely horrifying and heart-breaking. I keep calling, but no one is answering. All the lines are cut off. I'm going out of my mind.

By the evening, however, I do manage to speak to my family. I'm hesitant to go now. Perhaps this is not such a good time to visit...

When he hears about my hesitation, he gets very angry and wants me to stick to my plans. I can see that he wants to get rid of me, but I don't seem to understand why.

As I struggle with all these tormenting thoughts in the kitchen, I suddenly feel like calling my mom again. I pick the phone in the bedroom, and before I can dial, I hear him talking to someone on the phone, "I've found this girl and I want to take her out! Could you lend me your car?"

The other person replies, "No, you shouldn't do this! If Rebecca finds out, it won't be pretty!"

I hang up and barge into our living room and confront him, the right way. He keeps saying, "You misunderstood the whole thing! It's not what you think!"

I hear in my head, "You are weak! You don't count! Be quiet! Stand on the side! You do not amount to anything."

I continue packing.

The Next Day

He drives me to the airport. His body language clearly screams, "Just go! I don't care where. Just disappear, so I can breathe a little, so I can be free from this glue that is you!"

On the plane, I wonder, "Why can't he see how wonderful I am? Why does he want to be rid of me?"

~~~~

I am flying with Pakistan airlines. There are several stops before my destination. The first stop is in Karachi. At the checkpoint in Karachi, I find myself chatting with a middle-aged lady who seems to be very kind and caring.

She asks me, "Are you married?"

"Yes! I am."

"Is your husband good?"

"Yes, he is wonderful, really wonderful."

She looks at me for a moment and says, "If someone in your family asks you about your husband, just say he is ok."

I nod and look away quickly.

Meeting Mom and Dad Again

In this busy international airport, there are people everywhere. People are waiting to meet loved ones they haven't seen for a long time. Some are waiting with flowers.

I walk impatiently through the luggage check-out and then passport control. I stand in line to get my passport stamped, trying to look and see if mom and dad are on the other side.

At last, I get out, and immediately, I see dad standing in front of me, but he is looking away, he doesn't see me.

"Dad?"

"Oh? Are you here? I didn't see you!"

"Where is mom?"

"She went to find a place to buy flowers for you. Let's go and find her."

"Are you ok, dad?"

"Yes, my daughter."

"Oh, there's mom!"

Mom walks toward us and laughs at the same time, realising that she missed seeing me come out. She still does not have a flower in her hand, as usual.

"Let's go, the car's waiting to take us to our city."

We have to drive for six hours to get to the north. Dad is sitting in front. My mom is in the back seat with me.

Mom puts her arm around me, and, for a moment, I rest my head on her shoulder.

I think, "I don't feel relaxed. I feel stiff. It's so uncomfortable. I look like I would rather sit on the other side by myself."

And then, I gently pull myself away, looking forward to getting home and eating all the yummy foods I know my mother has prepared for me.

It's nice to be in my parents' home, although I feel like a guest, which I am now. It's nice to be with my sister and two younger brothers, eating all the wonderful food mom makes and watching our favourite movies like before.

Overall, there is negative energy in the air after the damage and misery caused by the earthquake. Everyone also notices that

I'm not happy, wondering with their worried eyes what is going on. But every time they try to find out what is really going on, I assure them that my husband is the best thing that has happened to me.

After One Month, I Am Back in Copenhagen

He seems happy to see me.

One evening, we are invited to visit my friend and her boyfriend. My friend doesn't hesitate to tell off her boyfriend right then, despite our being there, because he speaks to her in an annoyed tone of voice in front of us.

She yells, "Stop it right away and speak properly!"

I'm impressed, and I wish I could be more like her.

Nausea

I'm on the bathroom floor, my head in the toilet, throwing up. He is outside the bathroom, upset. We are in the middle of our usual fight, where I beg him to love me, and he tries as hard as he can to push me away. I run to the bathroom because I feel sick. After throwing up, I wash my mouth and face and come out.

He is still upset but not yelling anymore. He looks at me and says, "I'm warning you! Do not make the mistake of getting pregnant with me!"

Tonsillectomy

I'm busy with school, work, home, exercise and friends.

My tonsils are giving me trouble, and the doctor suggests I get them taken out. I have to be in hospital for two days. During visiting hours, he is there. The nurse asks me if I need a glass of juice.

I answer, "Yes!"

The nurse leaves the room. He starts laughing and says, "Don't think this is what's waiting for you at home!"

I look at him and smile bitterly, thinking, "How does one even respond to a comment like this?"

I keep quiet, but it has pinched me to hear his comment.

I wonder, "Would it be so terrible for him to be sweet to someone just for the sake of being sweet?"

I seem completely unaware of the fundamental truth about how impossible it is to love someone dearly when it is by force, and not knowing that, what I'm pursuing constantly isn't love at all, it's smallness and neediness.

Truly, true love doesn't look like this at all…

~~~

All my visitors leave, and I'm in bed, sitting by myself. My hospital roommate still has visitors. I don't want to disturb them and try not to look at them. I'm deep in my thought, trying to appear as if I'm ok being by myself. I'm obviously not doing a very good job because a woman who's visiting my roommate comes by my bed and tucks me under my quilt.

She looks like she's feeling sorry for me!

A Week Later

I'm sitting in the living room, early afternoon, watching a program on TV and eating nuts. He sits next to me, tickles me a bit and makes funny noises.

I'm extremely annoyed. I repeatedly ask him to stop, but he continues. Something is boiling inside me. I'm furious, and he still doesn't stop. I throw all the nutshells right into his face with all my strength, with a half-screaming sound that I don't recognise myself.

I'm shocked by my reaction, and he is shocked by my sudden outburst. He stands up and leaves the flat. When he returns, after what seems like a very long half hour, I apologise for my behaviour. I seem ashamed of and surprised at myself. Here I am, begging him always to be nice to me, and now when he does try, I do something like this.

He seems calmer now and asks me to never do this again—throwing things in his face.

The Next Day

I'm taking the train to visit my friend in Nordby, a small city in Southern Denmark. I'm looking forward to this as I always feel good around my childhood friend. We do absolutely nothing, yet it's fun to be with her.

My childhood friend has a friend. She finds fault with me all the time. She comments on what I wear, interrupts me when I want to say something, and when we go over to her house, I feel very unwelcome. I go there anyway!

I wonder, "Why is it like this? Wherever I go, this seems to follow me. People don't like me. Why is it like this? I wish it was different."

Venice

It is so magically beautiful and peaceful here! I'm sitting in this little homely restaurant on the edge of a narrow street and munching on spaghetti with Bolognese Sauce, and am drowned in my thoughts.

I feel the breeze and the warmth of the sun on my face. It's just perfect.

I think, "If this were to be the very last moment of my life, I would be ok with it. I feel one with everything in this particular moment that is so perfect, so free of fault."

I tell him, "We should stay over here tonight, in Venice!"

He replies, "I agree!"

After lunch, we walk around and check the hotels. He says, "It's too expensive. We should take the train and go back to our charter hotel in Rimini. It's already paid for."

I'm left with a feeling of unfinished-ness in Venice. I really want to stay here, but I say nothing.

On the way to the train station, I stop and lean over one of the many bridges, looking at the passing of tiny boats, thinking and repeating over and over again, "One day, I will come back here with someone I love. I will come back one day with someone I love..."

Birthday Gift

It's his birthday today. I'm overexcited. I want to buy something for him, something that I know he will use and appreciate. It's still winter and cold. I think, "A pair of gloves!"

I'm meeting him for lunch in a Chinese restaurant in the

centrum. Tingling with excitement, I hand the gift to him. He doesn't look happy. He still looks like he would rather be anywhere else but here. Reluctantly, he opens the bag and sees the gloves. He certainly doesn't look happy or excited over his birthday gift!

Usually, people pretend that they like the gift when they receive one. Not him. I hope that he'll smile and say 'thank you' sometime soon.

He says, "I don't need these gloves. Take them to the store, and get the money back!"

It's the *most* awkward birthday lunch I've ever experienced with anyone. I don't know what I should say or do. I am stunned by his reaction and words.

"Thank God it is only the two of us here and no one else to see my total embarrassment and humiliation," I think, even as my face is flushed hot with embarrassment.

Winter Holiday

Everyone travels to London during the Christmas season for their amazing sales. We have been here for a week and barely done any shopping. But we have seen some famous places that everyone goes to when they first visit London.

I find myself frozen now. I can't move, and it's not because of the cold weather. I just heard him say to me, "It's never fun to be with you! I don't have fun when I'm around you."

I stop walking. We are in the area around London Bridge. When I hear him saying this, I can't walk anymore. I feel frozen. He continues walking, not noticing that I've stopped. I see one English guy staring at me, possibly wondering, "What's wrong with her?"

I don't know what to do. Somehow, I feel I can't go on with all this *any*more. I don't know what else to do, what else to say.

That Night

We are at dinner with some of his friends. Everyone is talking. I'm quiet.

The waiter asks me, "What would you like to eat?"

I turn my head toward him, and ask, "Can I eat this buttered bread?"

Everyone looks surprised, and I can see that they all are uncomfortable. *I* seem to be surprised. Why did I need to ask for permission to order something for myself? It is something that bothers me, just under the surface.

As we go on, I seem to step down lower and lower. I seem to be available for any mistreatment and insult. A total doormat. And even when no one is putting me down, I ask for that lower position myself. I seem to not know how else to be.

Sohrab Sepehri

My sister, Tara, is here to visit us. Many years have passed since we last met. We are seeing each other again, and meeting her is really nice. She is very easy to talk to about everything. It *is* nice to have her around.

We get busy talking about the Iranian poet, Sohrab Sepehri.

She reads this poem to me,

I'm a Muslim.
My Kiblah is a red rose,
The river is where I stand to pray,

The light is what I put my head on while prostrating…
The desert is where I stand to pray…
I wash my body with the heartbeat of the windows…

I laugh hysterically. Tara stops reading the poem and asks me, surprised, "What?"

I answer, still giggling, "This Sohrab Sepehri, his writing is total nonsense, don't you think? Who published his book?"

Tara asks, "Why do you say that?"

I reply, laughing, "What was he smoking? 'The heartbeat of the windows?'"

Tara simply smiles and puts the book down. We carry on doing other things.

The Café Guy

Hunger makes you do things you normally don't do. Emotional hunger takes you to places and encounters that you'll come to regret for a long time. Sometimes for the rest of your life.

~~~~

I meet a guy in a café near my home. How did I notice him? I can't even remember.

We just get busy talking. We sit down and have a cup of tea and my favourite apple-pie.

He says, "I can read palms. Do you want me to tell you things about you that I know?"

Totally interested, I ask him eagerly to read my palm. He smiles and takes my hand, and, after a few seconds, he smiles again.

I ask, curious, "What?"

He answers, "You are going to be my girlfriend!"

I look up, surprised by what I have just heard, but I am indeed flattered that he is showing an interest in me.

I leave the café with a smile on my face, and keep looking at his number written down on a sticky note from the café. I think, "Shall I call him?"

I'm on night shift tonight and am happy that I won't be interacting with my husband. I am fed up of and with him.

During my night shift, I call the café guy and speak to him a couple of times through the night. We arrange to meet early in the morning as soon as my shift finishes.

It is seven in the morning. I take the tram to the café guy's place and stay a couple of hours. On the way home in the tram, after those carefree and not-giving-a-damn two hours, I'm ok with what I've done. I feel no remorse at all. I don't seem to care about anything anymore.

At Home

He is awake and asks, "Why are you so late?"

I answer shortly, "Too much to do at work."

He looks at me as if he notices something is different. I am too annoyed to talk to him. I wish I didn't have to. I'm fed up with *everything* about him.

Later That Evening

I take two suitcases filled with my clothes and leave. I take a taxi to my "friend," the guy I've known for less than forty-eight hours.

The Beginning of the End

I call him and tell him, "I'm not coming back anymore."

In disbelief, he argues with me on the phone. I just hang the phone up. I don't want to hear anything he says.

One of my friends calls me and tells me, "He is completely out of his mind, crying non-stop. We know he deserves this, since he has always treated you so badly. But still, we feel sorry for him. Is there any way you can change your mind and come back?"

I remember all those times that he repeatedly told me that he didn't want to be with me, and he didn't want the gift from me, and he didn't enjoy being around me.

I answer firmly and surely, "No!"

My friend continues, "What you are doing isn't 'good', but it will teach him a lesson and certainly will teach all the other useless guys something too!"

The New Life

Since we have no children, thank God, the divorce happens very smoothly, via mail.

It's been one month, and I've been having the time of my life. I go to work every day, and the rest of the time, I have a good time with my new friend. The only thing I do not think about is what was. I'm happy with things now. The rest doesn't matter. My older sister and all my friends are very supportive about all this.

The Second Month

I meet my ex-husband by accident in a grocery store near where I stay. Perhaps he's been following me. He walks past me and looks at me angrily with tears in his eyes, but we exchange no words. I'm moved, although truly, I would rather not see him ever again.

Somehow, the picture of his tearful eyes doesn't leave my mind. Although I feel bad for him, it does make me wonder, "Why?"

I'm completely puzzled.

For more than five years, I have been insulted, belittled and unwanted by him. Now that I have given him what he always wanted, why is he shedding all these crocodile tears? Should he not be happy he is finally rid of me? He didn't enjoy being with me anyway!

I guess pushing away is easy and good, but not being pushed away…

Possessive

Looks like wherever I go, trouble and unrest find me. It looks like no matter who I am with, there are always lots of arguments and fights.

I notice that something is not right with my new Prince Charming either. When we go out, he gets into fights with people over trivial things.

I want to go out with friends, go to the gym and out for coffees, and he always wants to be around. He is stuck to me like glue. Every time he behaves this way, I realise how bad and annoying it is to have someone stick to you like glue. I think, "Oh my God, I can see how unattractive it is to be like this! Like glue! I was always like this with my ex."

The Ending

The story with the café guy comes to an end, as it is impossible to continue like this. I need some breathing space. So I move back, temporarily, to my sister's home again.

He continues to terrorise me for a while, following me wherever I go. He calls and threatens. He comes and knocks on my sister's door in the middle of the night. I feel nervous all the time, realising how stupid I've been.

~~~

It's the middle of the night, and he is outside, banging on the door. I look at my sister, my whole body shaking uncontrollably.

I feel the trembling in every pore of my body as if a billion creepy-crawlies are running through my veins and running through my bones. I feel restless and afraid. My whole body feels on the edge. I think, "What have I done? How stupid can one be? I wish someone had told me the consequences of moving in with someone you don't know. I wish someone had told me that if something or someone appears to be too good to be true, it's simply not true!"

I have to take a sedative in order to sleep. How stupid can one be? How could one think that a quick fix like this would be ideal?

The Next Morning

I decide to travel and visit my parents again until things cool down.

The night before travelling, I meet my ex in McDonalds to sort out some money issues. There are many tears and a lot of crying and regretting! Although it's over between us, we seem to be more bound now than we were during our entire five years of marriage, perhaps because of the surge of all this guilt.

We say goodbye, and I leave the country.

First Time in Qatar

Visiting my parents is great. I get to rest a lot. I feel safe here, away from all the dramas in my life.

I visit an old friend, and I start talking to her about how I failed in my marriage. I feel sad and ashamed for not succeeding. Tears roll down my cheeks and, suddenly, in the midst of my painful memories, I feel something that doesn't feel like it is from this world. I remember having experienced the same serene feeling when I was in my aunt's wooden house in my younger days…

~~~~

After a week, I decide to take a five-day trip to Qatar. I plan to visit a couple of hospitals to see if I can get a job there.

Nothing seems appealing, so I enjoy my time for five days and come back.

After Two Months

I return to Copenhagen and go back to living with my sister again.

Working and exercising is all I do. It's not easy to go back and live with someone else when you have already been independent. So living with my sister isn't easy for me anymore. I can also feel that my sister is quite fed up with me.

She asks me to move out. I agree, but I need to live somewhere, and I know neither where nor how. So I contact my ex to finalise the money issue for the flat we owned together.

Back with the Ex

The meeting is unexpectedly pleasant, but since he doesn't have the money to pay my share, he promises to help me find a rented room somewhere in the area until we sell the flat.

The next day, we meet again and go room-hunting, and after half-a-day of spending time on possibly the weirdest people renting rooms in the city of Copenhagen, I am fed up.

He suggests, "Why don't you come back and live in your own flat? We could be flat-mates?"

I'm surprised by the suggestion, but think for a moment and answer, "Yes, maybe I should. I'll come with my suitcases tomorrow!"

Six Months Pass

We are back together and doing excellent, like never before. We decide to move to the US for his music school. Within a few months, we sell everything and travel to California, hoping for a fresh start, with no audiences to observe all our moves and waiting for our dramas to take off again.

~~~~

Not many weeks pass, however, until I realise things are back to our old normal again. Nothing I do is right and he is upset most of the time, remembering that I left him for that café guy.

Once again, I feel lonely, stuck and very unhappy. At least, back in Copenhagen, I had my job. Now I have nothing but my old friends—arguments, fights and unhappiness. I am left with the feeling of not knowing what to do. Yet again.

An old saying echoes in my head,

"Never go back, even if you could."

The Best Moment in the Last Five Months

My best moment in the last five months has been receiving a letter from my childhood friend. I cycle to the lake nearby. I want to have a peaceful moment with my friend's letter. I finish reading the letter and shed a lot of tears.

The Veranda in California-The Voice

Night after night, I sit on the veranda and try to ignore what I repeatedly hear from the deepest of my inner depths, "Just go! Please leave! Just take the first step, I'll show you the rest of the way. Don't be afraid! You can start afresh!"

I am still here, sitting on the terrace in our home in California. I look at the sky, waiting for a sign or something, hoping for giant hands to come down from heaven and rescue me from all the mess I've made in my life.

I am tired of wishing that he would die, so I can be free from my own weakness. I've reached a point with him that I even hate the way he speaks, the way he eats, the way he talks, the way he walks.

I am sitting on the porch, deep in my thoughts, when, out of nowhere, I see myself holding something in my hands. I glance at the image for a second, seeing a book in my hands, and I hear a voiceless voice, "You've written this book!

Just leave!

Take the first step and go back!

Just go!"

I walk inside and tell him that I will leave him the next morning.

He is surprised with my sudden decision and tries to talk me out of it. He is hugging me and crying and begging me not to go. He leads his act into forcefully sleeping with me. I feel sorry for him, and sorry for myself for letting things reach this stage. I don't say stop, even though I want to scream, "Stop!"

Suddenly, I seem to enter a very strange state—feeling cold, heartbreakingly blank! I think, "I just want to die! I can't do this anymore!"

It seems that even *I* can't tolerate my doormat behaviour anymore!

I hear a disturbing female voice in my head,

"The only way to get out of this mess, and the only way for you to be free, is to just kill yourself. Did you hear that? Kill yourself now. There is no hope for you. All you need is to go to the kitchen and use a knife."

Feeling scared and estranged, I start weeping, "Please leave me alone. I am not feeling good at all!"

Realising, by looking at me, that something is seriously wrong, he says, "Go! The hell with me! Please don't look like this. Just go!"

I get up, go to the bathroom and take a shower.

~~~~

I get up in the early hours of the morning, take my suitcases out of the closet, and manage to put all I own into three big and two small suitcases.

He looks worried! He is sitting in the living room, observing every single move I make.

The flight back to Copenhagen isn't until late at night, but I just need to get out so that I'm not reminded any more about how I have wasted seven years of my life and how I will never get that time back.

At least after the divorce on paper, I should have known better. As a famous Persian saying suggests,

"One could predict a good year by its spring."

I should have known…

Yellow Cab Driver

I drag my suitcases down the stairs, one at a time, trying not to stumble. I manage to get everything to the side of the road, and I wave out to a yellow cab.

I smile. The warm breeze of LA on my naked shoulders feels amazingly comforting. A yellow cab pulls up in front of me. The driver steps out to help me with the suitcases.

"Could you take me to the Metropolitan Motel please?"

The driver pauses for a brief moment, and he looks at me while sorting my cases in the trunk of his car.

I ask, "Do you know where Metropolitan Motel is?"

"Yes, I do, but are you sure you want to go there?"

"Yes!"

The driver insists, "I know another motel, a bit further down the road, but more suitable for you. Metropolitan is mostly a place for prostitutes."

He mentions the word 'prostitute' very quietly, as if he doesn't want to mention the word 'prostitute' in front of me at all.

Totally embarrassed about not knowing where I was heading, I look down, nod and say, "Thank you!"

Back in Copenhagen

It's great to be back. Seeing my sister and her children is good. Once again, until I find my own place, I'm staying with my sister.

Lucky

I find an apartment, ready for me to move in, just within a couple of days. I feel very lucky. My sister and my new brother-in-law help me buy all the furniture in only one day from IKEA.

Housewarming Gift

My new place is special. From the moment I enter it, I feel accompanied. I feel I have people around me, and I am not alone. It's a place with good energy!

This is the first night I'm sleeping in this apartment, in this bed. This is the first time, after so many years that I'm sleeping alone.

The smell of my brand-new bed, the brand-new sheets feels great.

It's the middle of the night.

I dream I'm sitting on my brand-new bed, with its brand-new sheets. From the wall opposite the bed, a tall woman—with long golden hair flowing over her shoulders and dressed in white, along with six others behind her, appears. I can only, and barely, see the face of the lady in front.

I wonder, "What's happening? Am I dreaming? Who are these guys? Why aren't I running? Why am I not scared? I should be as there are seven strangers in my bedroom!"

The lady in white speaks, "Do not worry, Rebecca! We are here with you. We will take care of you!"

I wake up and find myself lying in bed, smiling at the peculiar dream I just had.

I think, "This is the best housewarming gift!"

Living Life

Life can't be better than this. I have my job back, and I am living in my own place. I feel free, and I feel happy. Everything seems possible. One of my co-workers asks me out for coffee one day, and I agree without any hesitation. The coffee turns into dinner, and I enjoy every single minute of it.

My date is a very well-spoken and pleasant guy, he is an actor with parts in theatre plays. He paints, and his absolute favourite hobby is reading books. I ask him about his painting, and he tells me all about the techniques and the kinds of colours he usually uses.

Suddenly he stops, smiles and says joyfully, "I should paint you! You have the perfect features for a painting—black hair, beautiful face, great glow. Please, would you allow me to do a painting of you?"

I blush when I hear this, smile in disbelief and look at him one more time to detect any signs of ridicule or joking.

"No, he isn't making fun of me, he isn't… He means what he just said."

I smile again. He notices my surprised facial expression, and says, "Oh my God, you've never heard this before? No one has ever told you this before?"

I smile again. I don't know what to say and how to answer. After dinner, he walks with me across the city to take me home!

In bed, I think about him and what he said earlier. He thinks I'm beautiful.

This is, indeed, the first time I have heard someone say *so* many nice things about me.

After a Week

He asks me, "What kind of relationship would you want to have with me? Because I don't want to be in a serious relationship with anyone."

We are on the tram. We had just had lunch together. I'm disappointed and a little confused. I wish I could continue seeing him. He says something else that makes me wonder what he means, "We all need to find ourselves first before getting involved with someone else."

What he just said sounds very profound and deep, but I don't get it and don't dare to ask what he means. I remain quiet, sitting next to him on the tram. We kiss goodbye, and he gets off.

I feel like someone who has lost something valuable, and think, "Sounds nice, finding oneself. How does one do this?"

Uplifting Words

Later, when my sister finds out about this break up, she is very surprised and asks, "What do you do that no one stays with you?"

My brother-in-law smiles and nods in agreement.

At this point, I am still unaware of the sad cultural undercurrent that runs among the majority of people on our planet, where constantly pointing out mistakes, seeing fault, correcting and criticising—rather than encouraging and educating—are the most normal norm of all.

I don't say anything, but think, "My sister is right. Why is it like this? Something must be wrong with the way I am."

So one blind person agrees to being led by another blind person…

The Perfect Guy

Since I'm not capable of keeping the guys I pick, my sister fixes a date for me with one of her classmates, supposedly a very nice guy—a perfect dating match. I agree to meet him.

I meet him in a restaurant downtown, and from the first moment we shake hands, I notice that he is very polite and educated and, for some reason, this makes me very uncomfortable.

We order food and while waiting for it, we get busy talking about our jobs. The wine is served now, and we are about to say cheers, when he puts his wine glass on the floor in front of my feet and says, "For your health!"

I'm surprised and ask him, "What does this mean?"

He answers, "In ancient times in Persia, this is what they did to cheer with someone who's worthy. It basically means, 'You are so worthy that I'm willing to be the ground you walk on, and therefore I salute the ground that you are walking on.'"

I smile and think, "What a sweet tale! What a sweet guy! He knows nice stories."

Our time at dinner passes pleasantly, and we say goodbye.

I know for sure that I never want to meet him again.

It seems I don't like "nice."

Fast and Able

I work almost every day. I'm filled with energy and the word 'tired' doesn't exist in my vocabulary. Mostly, I feel that 24 hours aren't enough for all I want to do in a day.

The phone rings, and I realise without answering that I must have overslept. I answer the phone and say, "I'm on my way!

Sorry!"

I jump on my bicycle, and it takes me forty minutes to get to work. I love riding my bicycle, especially in the rain, with my raincoat and my music on my Walkman. Life couldn't be better!

When I enter the unit, everyone is surprised that I got there so fast. Every day, I feel proud of being so able.

Greece

I am going to a party island in Greece with my friend. I meet a charming Greek bartender. Very soon, I'm head over heels in love with him, and he pays attention to me all the time. At one point, he says, "You look like the ancient queen, Cleopatra!"

I'm overwhelmed by his comment. I've never heard such a nice comment in my entire life.

A Week Later

We are leaving the island, but I wish I could stay here forever. I don't want to leave!

Three Months Later

I convince my friend to travel to Greece again. She agrees. We arrive in Greece, and the first thing I do is meet him. We have a great time together. Again. Before leaving, I invite him to come to Denmark to visit and stay with me.

A Few Months Later

He is coming. I pay for his ticket because he says he doesn't have money, and I am embarrassed to tell anyone about this. My older sister knows about this somehow, and she makes sure I know that she knows.

I don't care. I just feel happy he is coming, in spite of my paying for the ticket and all. I think, "Oh, what fun we'll have together."

~~~

We arrive home from the airport. I prepare a large dinner because my sisters are also coming over. He says, "My luggage was stolen at the airport, and, therefore, I have nothing else to wear."

I assure him, "Don't worry! We will go shopping tomorrow!"

He only has a saxophone with him which he says he needs to practice most times every day. Dinner with him and my family is delightful, and we have a great time the whole evening.

The Next Day

I take him shopping, feeling awkward, but he looks very happy and very comfortable. Whatever we buy looks great on him. He is a very handsome guy.

The Third Day

He asks me, "Did you touch my saxophone? It's broken! You must have touched it and broken it."

I don't like the way he speaks to me, and I don't like it that he is accusing me of breaking his saxophone, and, above all, I *don't* like the feeling that he is making this story up.

The Month Passes

It is time for him to leave. I'm sad that he is leaving, and at the same time, I'm annoyed by the fact that I have to give him money to take home until he finds a job.

I don't like the feeling of paying for him at all. I feel like I'm buying him.

~~~

From this time on, every six months, I travel to meet him in different islands of Greece. Wherever we go and stay, I'm the one who pays for everything. I pretend I'm happy about it.

Well, I am still happy to be with him.

Yes, it's very obvious, as Malcom X said,

"If you don't stand for something, you'll fall for anything."

On the Island of Mykonos

After travelling around at my expense for ten days, I get up to go to the bathroom one morning, and when I return, he is sitting by the bed, looking all grumpy.

I try to cheer him up by smiling at him. This attempt is interrupted when he spits right at me.

I get shocked and scream, "What are you doing? Why did you do such a thing?"

He smiles and nonchalantly apologises, but I'm heartbroken over his behaviour. I'm very sad that he doesn't see me as that ancient Cleopatra anymore, otherwise he would not act like this.

I stay with him for four more days in Greece, and the day I'm travelling back, I start crying at the airport. I tell him, "I will miss you!"

He remains silent!

The Smile

November is called the suicide month in Denmark.

I get up very early every morning to get the 7:10 tram to work.

I sit down next to the window and observe the view outside with all the yellow lights that are trying, the best they can, to cut through the morning darkness of the city. Crumpled together and heads down in the tram, everyone is trying to warm up and trying to ignore the cold and the dark outside. The tram is approaching the next stop, and as a habit, I observe everyone who is getting ready to leave the tram and eagerly look to see who steps into the tram instead.

A well-dressed lady with light brown hair steps into the tram. For an instant, our eyes meet, and she smiles at me. In a tram full of sleepy folks with their heads down, and where no one has acknowledged another, her smile—like a warm breeze—caresses my whole body. I automatically smile back. She turns to the right side of the tram and sits down.

I feel lifted, and a sensation of warmth takes over my entire body. I'm happy and in a good mood with a big smile on my face. I look out through the window of the tram.

It's still dark and cold, but now, it looks beautiful in my eyes.

While looking out from the tram, I'm reminded of a story my dad used to tell us many years ago.

The Shepherd and the Lion

Once there was a shepherd who used to go into the desert every night. He would sit down and eat his dinner while his sheep were around, not so far from his sight.

One night, an old lion was passing by and asked the shepherd if he could sit and have dinner with him. The shepherd gladly invited the lion to sit and share his dinner. While they were both eating, the shepherd got annoyed by the noisy and untidy way the lion was eating. He couldn't refrain himself from commenting, "Hey, could you eat nicely without making so much noise? Could you eat properly please?"

The lion looked at the shepherd for a couple of seconds, then said, "Please, could you take your dagger and hit my head with it?"

The shepherd, who was surprised, refused to do what the lion was asking him, but the lion persisted and kept saying, "Please do it! It's for your own good! Please, just one cut on my head!"

The shepherd, however reluctant, decided to do it just to get the lion off his back. He hit the lion's head with the dagger and blood spurted out from the cut. The shepherd worriedly said, "I didn't really want to…"

And before he finished his sentence, the lion stood on all fours, said thank you for dinner and left.

Many months passed, and once again, the lion came across the shepherd who was sitting in the same spot and eating his dinner as usual. The lion asked if he could join him and the shepherd accepted, remembering the last time.

"Do you remember the cut I asked you to hit my head with the dagger?"

Embarrassed, the shepherd nodded and said, "I didn't really want to do that!"

"Don't worry about that, I asked you to do that, but please do me a favour now! Could you come here and look at the area where you hit my head with the dagger?"

The shepherd took a step toward the lion and searched for the signs of the cut on the lion's head.

"I can't find it. It's gone, it's healed."

The lion smiled and said, "Yes, the cut on my head healed after that night, but the sore you caused, by telling me that I was eating badly, is still fresh in my heart."

I find myself whispering, "Yes, a sore in the heart may never heal, but a simple warm smile can be healing and stay with you for a long time!"

From the bottom of my heart, I wish—for that smiling lady in the tram—the best of the best in life...

Naïve

Overall, life feels good. I enjoy my freedom and my independence. Sometimes I feel lonely because my Greek love affair ended like a Greek tragedy.

On the tram, on the way back home one day, I meet one of my sister's old friends who was frequently invited to their place when I lived with them years ago. We make small talk, and he says that he has recently divorced his wife.

Before I leave the tram, he asks, "Why don't you come by my

place next week for a cup of tea? Both of our birthdays are next week. We could celebrate together."

I think, "Why not?"

And continue, "Sure, I will come by. I'll bring a cake!"

The Following Week

I'm in his home, sitting politely in the living room, waiting for my tea. He comes with the tea and cake and sits next to me, a bit too close. I feel awkward.

I'm about to take a sip from the tea, and he comes even closer, to the point that I feel *really* uncomfortable.

My body language is shouting clearly that I'm not happy with whatever intention he has in mind. He puts his hand around my shoulder and says, "Don't feel shy, it is ok!"

I stand up and say in an angry tone, yet as politely as I can, "I didn't come here for this!"

I'm realising how stupid I really am. Cursing myself, I think, "What else is he supposed to think when you come to his home? Why in the world would I want to meet him anyway? Were we friends before? Did we ever get along? How stupid and naive am I? I should leave!"

I stand up and walk toward the door. "No, don't go please! Come and finish your tea!"

I feel sorry for him because he seems regretful of his dumb behaviour. Reluctantly, I sit down and finish my tea.

Twenty Minutes Pass

We leave his home, take the tram to go somewhere for a drink. In the tram, on the way, he says, "Don't tell this to your sister!"

At the pub, I have one drink, and then I go home.

Only on the way home do I realise what has happened. I feel sick remembering how disrespectful he was toward me by thinking about doing what he was thinking to do. I feel totally stupid for going there to his place and then continuing to sit there after his insulting suggestion.

I reach home and still feel completely beside myself. I really need to tell someone what has happened. I call my childhood friend, and, unfortunately, the answering machine comes on. I leave this message for her, half crying, "I wish you would answer! I need to speak to you. Something bad has happened, and I feel very sad. Please call me when you get this!"

All alone, I cry myself to sleep, wondering, "WHY? Why is it that whoever passes my way is totally disrespectful of me? Why is all this happening to me? Something must be seriously wrong with me!"

All these tormenting thoughts make me feel even worse. I need help. I'm hurting, and I don't want to hurt.

I find myself in a world where being spontaneous is considered as gullibility and naiveté, and therefore, I am stepped all over and taken for granted. Sadly, it seems like no one misses the golden opportunity of taking advantage of a total fool.

I certainly don't know how to handle the world I live in.

Suddenly, I remember the woman in the tram with her smile. Remembering her kind face and her warm smile makes my tears flow out like a river of sorrow. My pillow is wet with my tears, but remembering her smile and the memory of that happy moment, for an instant, makes me forget about my horrible experience earlier this evening.

I fall asleep in the end.

The Next Day

Early in the morning, my childhood friend calls. She says, "The way you were speaking on the answering machine, I really thought you were raped or something. Thank God you are okay! Forget about this idiot. You didn't do anything wrong! He is an asshole, that's all. Take a train and come to me this weekend!"

I feel much better after speaking to my friend. My childhood friend means so much to me. She is truly the only saving grace in my life.

I do get ready and go to work, but last night's memory is with me all through, even as I perform my duties at work. I follow the doctor for the daily round. As we enter the room of the patient, he introduces himself and then introduces me to the patient, "And this is our nurse today!"

The patient, who is a sixty-five-year-old woman with chronic pain, says, "Oh, really? For a moment I thought Queen Silvia of Sweden walked into the room with you!"

The doctor smiles, gives me an admiring glance, and answers, "Yes, Queen Silvia decided to work with us today!"

I smile! Their comments warm my heart, and, at the same time, I think, "How come no one noticed Queen Silvia in me last night?"

I straighten myself, remembering the marvellous compliment I heard a few moments ago, and with that, I continue with the round.

Destiny

Sometimes, in life, we need to choose from the several choices that have been put in our lap, and it's amazing when that happens. Sometimes, we have to choose between two things that we love. I find myself in one such moment now.

I am in-between two amazing choices. I've been offered a spot in midwifery school in a city near where my childhood friend lives and also offered a job in the Far East, where the sun will always shine.

Both of these letters are in my hand on the same day.

I'm tempted to stay and study to become a midwife, but I'm also crazy about going somewhere with sunshine all-year round.

After a Week

I decide to travel to the sunny Far East, but first things first, I'm going to take the train to my friend before I leave to work for a year.

I visit my sister before the train trip and tell her about the incident with their old friend. She looks at me with a mix of ridicule and annoyance, and says, "You deserve this! How many thousand times must I pull you out from the trouble you get yourself in? I'm so tired that you don't get it. You deserve it. I'm happy this happened to you so you can finally understand."

I make the mistake of telling my sister what happened to me. I seem totally unaware of this Divine knowing yet, that,

> "A dead and non-burning candle is not able to provide warmth or reinforce life in anything or anyone."

And yet, I keep making the same mistake over and over again.

Burdened by all these harsh words I hear, the lack of support and empathy from my sister, and with a still-alive and heavy feeling in my heart at the memory of that night, I go home and pack. I have to take the train very early the next morning.

I'm still sad on my way to the train station. I cry on the train. I cry for eight hours straight. I don't care if anyone is seeing me. I listen to the song of the Swedish singer, Orup, "Regn hos mej",

I heard on Radio
that there will be sun today
But it sounds very strange
I have only rain with me...

I cry nonstop, for the wound caused by disappointment and my unreasonable expectations.

I reach my friend's home, my eyes so puffy that she notices immediately. When I tell her what happened, she hugs me and says, "I understand how you feel!"

We have a very good time together for a week, but now I have to say goodbye to my best friend for a year. It isn't easy but needs to be done.

My friend wonders, "I don't get it! How can you think about going somewhere else and start from zero again?"

"I feel something is calling me! I have to go. Do not worry, I will be back in one year!"

Moved Again

There are times in one's life when it seems necessary to stay wherever you are. And then there come times in one's life when it becomes necessary to move on. Life will take care of this for us.

It looks like the time has come for me to continue my life's journey elsewhere, even though I don't seem to know about this myself yet.

~~~~

I put all my furniture in a rented storage unit in Copenhagen, and with the arranged flight from the hospital in Doha, in the Far East, I arrive to an already arranged housing, thinking I will be back in a year.

April

It's already thirty plus degrees here. Each morning, when I wake up, I hurry up and walk straight toward the window, taking a quick peek to see if it's still sunny outside.

I notice that most people, who come to this country to work, already have a friend or family member here. I came on my own, all by myself. I'm SO proud of myself.

After a Month

The sun is shining all the time here.

I've stopped wondering if it's going to be sunny today. I now know for sure that the sun will be showing up every day.

I'm far away from everything and everybody that is familiar to me, but I'm happy being where I am. I'm busy working in the hospital most days, and I go out with Luis, my new friend, on weekends.

After One Year

In the blink of an eye, one year has passed, and I decide to extend my contract for another year. Even though my work hours are too long and the forced night shifts aren't desirable at all, I'm happy being here. I realise that I indeed do very well when I'm alone. I do things better when I'm on my own. I do not do well at all when I'm living under someone else's shadow.

Six Years Later

Time moves fast, sometimes almost in a blur.

Bedtime

"Boys! Let's brush our teeth, it's our story time!"

Between leading my two little boys to the washroom and making sure they don't get other ideas instead of brushing, I make sure they go straight to bed. Finally, after a lot of giggling and a few attempts of trying to get away, my two boys are settled in bed. I'm in bed with them, and the boys snuggle on either side of me.

I suggest, "Shall we sing our usual bedtime songs?"

The younger one chimes in, "Yes!"

He is the one who enjoys the songs the most and knows all the words by heart. My other boy, older by two years, also sings along. He sometimes changes the rhyming text in a way he likes. We laugh a lot about this. I love our bedtime routine. After the singing session, I read stories to them.

"Ok guys, let me tell you this story that I know. I'm sure you'll like it. This is a good one, I promise! Listen now!

The Snake and the Shepherd

There was a time, long ago, when a very poor shepherd lived in a village. He had a few sheep that he took to the desert every night. One night, as he was sitting and watching his sheep, a snake came by and sat with him.

The shepherd was drinking milk that he took with him from home. He poured some of his milk in a small bowl and offered it to the snake.

They both drank their milk peacefully and enjoyed each other's company. After a while, when the snake wanted to leave, he spat a pearl into the empty bowl and said, before leaving, "Thank you for your kindness! The milk and your company mean the world to me!"

The shepherd was surprised and very happy. It was a real pearl, and he could sell it and get money for it.

From that night on, the snake and the shepherd met at their usual spot every night and drank their milk. The sheep wandered around—not so far away from them—grazing.

At the end of each nightly meeting, the snake would leave one pearl in the bowl for the shepherd before saying thank you and goodbye.

The shepherd became a wealthy businessman because of all these pearls he was receiving from the snake.

A while later, the shepherd desired to travel, and he told his son, "Go every night to the same place, sit with the snake and give the snake the milk!"

The son did as the father asked him, but after a few nights, he thought, "I could follow the snake, find his home, kill him and take all the pearls instead of waiting for one pearl every night. Tonight, I'm going to do this!"

That night, he followed the snake to his home. He lifted his dagger to smash the snake in the head. The snake, who was way sharper and faster than him, jumped, but the dagger cut his tail off, and at the same time, the snake bit him hard and deep, spreading his venom into the boy.

The shepherd's son died immediately.

The shepherd returned from the trip, and sadly, he found out that his son had been killed by his snake friend.

A few years passed, and one night, the shepherd went back to his old routine of walking his sheep to the desert. Sure enough, after a few nights, the snake came by. The shepherd offered to sit with him. After a long silence between the two old friends, the shepherd said to the snake, "I know what my son did, and I understand why you did what you did. Come! Let's forget about everything. Let's be friends again like old times!"

The snake looked at the shepherd for a moment, smiled, and then said, "Until the day I remember my lost tail and you remember your lost son, there won't be any friendship between us!"

As I shared the story with my boys, it dawned on me that we are not only what we are by ourselves. We are also who we are related to.

~~~~

I look at my sons who are fast asleep by now.

I leave their bedroom, and, for a moment, I get a very intense feeling of being lost.

I see myself as if I'm watching a movie. My mind is throwing these questions at me at the same time, "What am I doing here? Reading and making up these stories for these two little boys? Who are these boys? Who am I? What's my name?"

I am overpowered and dazzled by what I just experienced. For a moment, I stand there, my hand on the doorknob, totally stumped. As soon as I close the door behind me, I breathe, pause, and remember it all.

I wanted to explore the world. So I left the life I had in Denmark behind and came to Qatar.

At that time, the last thing on my mind was getting married again. I was definitely not thinking about having children. I was enjoying working at the hospital where I met my husband-to-be and, after about two years of dating, and one long break up, we were married.

~~~~

Our wedding was the talk of Doha.

Family members and friends from many parts of the world were there to celebrate our wedding.

Twelve days after the wedding, my family left, and I was left with an odd feeling.

I felt restless all the time. Something told me that I should go and visit my parents.

In the end, I convinced myself that I must be feeling homesick because I had just parted from them all. When we returned from our honeymoon, I was still struggling, in my mind, with that nagging feeling. Should I or shouldn't I go and visit my parents, even if just for a few days?

~~~~

One morning, I visited a friend. I just *had* to go and visit her. I needed to talk to her.

We sat and talked about everything—the wedding, the honeymoon and all. I mentioned what I had been feeling since the day my family left.

She asked, "Why don't you just go for a few days and come back?"

I thought for a moment and replied, "No, I'll just forget about it, we just have seen each other!"

After eating lunch with her, I went home.

Early Next Morning

My alarm clock went off. I had to get up and go to my computer course. I turned to one side to get up and saw my husband sitting up already, on the bed next to me. He asked gently, "Are you awake?"

I nodded but could tell something wasn't quite right. He said, "Your father passed away early yesterday morning and is already buried."

Stunned by what I just heard, the conversation with my

friend in the early hours of the day before flashed through my mind. I ran down the stairs to call my mom.

It was true. I wasn't dreaming. It was not a nightmare. It was true. The morning before—while I was chatting with my friend about going to visit my parents—my father was getting ready to go to work. He came down the stairs when, all of a sudden, he clasped his chest, fell on the ground and passed away.

Just like that!

Housemaid Number 15

Rose is saying, "I know how many housemaids you have changed so far, madame! Every day, everybody in the playground downstairs talks about you. You are so mean. All madams and sirs are mean. You all have money, and that is all. You people have nothing else. And if God didn't give you money, we would be on the same level as you. I don't understand why I have to take care of your damn children while my small children are being taken care of by my mother and sister, and not me. I hate this. I hate my life. I hate that you have everything, and I have to work for you!"

I look at her while she's having one of her usual moments. My mind flashes back to the day I was in the agency, when I saw her picture in her CV, and didn't like the cold and bitter look in her eyes.

I remember saying to myself, "Maybe it's just the picture."

Now that she is showering me with all her miserable comments, I keep quiet. I look at her and just listen, seeing that picture and that cold look in my mind. I know that there is nothing I can say or do. I know that I ignored what I saw that day and still chose her.

However, Rose's angry outburst takes me back to a time twelve years earlier, when my first housemaid arrived in our home.

Twelve Years Ago

In the airport, my mother is sitting, waiting to board. She is going to come and help me with my first baby. She is crying when a woman who is sitting next to her asks her, "What's the problem, sister?"

Mom answers, "My husband died ten months ago, and this is the first time I'm travelling alone without him."

Mom is still busy wiping her tears off her face, and she notices the woman's face twitching with annoyance. She looks like she wants to say something, but doesn't know if or how she should. The woman finally blurts out, "Aren't you free and comfortable now?"

In the midst of her tearfulness, she sees the woman's annoyed face, and actually hears what she is saying. My mom starts laughing out loud.

Almost Due

Jan is in her twenties—a petite, Christian girl from the Philippines. She arrives at our big villa when it is overflowing with visitors. We are all waiting for the arrival of my first baby.

After Jan's first night in the house, my mother asks, "Is Jan still here?"

While preparing breakfast, I say, "Yes! Why?"

Mother continues, "If I were Jan, I would've run away. There are so many guests and so much to do in this house!"

Everyone laughs and carries on setting the table for breakfast. Everything seems fine. Jan is a hardworking and energetic girl and is doing her job very well. The size, the 'bigness' of the house and the many chores that she has to do don't seem to bother her at all.

~~~

My baby boy is born, and, from the first moment, Jan is very fond of the baby. I have recurring dreams about Jan stealing my baby and replacing me in my home.

My house is still full of guests—my sisters, my mother and my in-laws. I feel tired and agitated all the time. I want to fall asleep, but I can't allow myself to. I constantly think, "What if I fall asleep and the baby wakes up?!"

It's nice to have everybody around, but I miss the usual quietness of my house. I miss having my husband relaxing next to me, instead of running around and hosting others all the time.

~~~

After three weeks, all the guests are gone, but my mother is still with me which is a great comfort.

One morning, when I'm sitting at the breakfast table, my mother comes and joins me, and I can see that she's crying. The memory of my father passing away is still fresh for her. In a couple of weeks, it will be one year. I'm not happy that my mother is sad. I want everyone to be happy now that I have a baby boy. I don't want to hear or see sadness.

I remember that all through my life, I have heard my mom complaining about my dad. She was never happy with him or with anything else, really. Something was wrong with everything. Always!

As if she can read my thoughts and memories in my eyes, she

cries more and says, "Earlier, I thought I had all these problems. I thought I was unlucky. Now I see I was very lucky and happy even with that stupid husband of mine. I had everything, and now that he is gone, I feel very unhappy and unlucky."

I feel sorry for my mom.

~~~~

My mother leaves after one month, and I start to feel sadness and mood swings. From morning to evening, all I feel like doing is finding fault with everything and everyone, and Jan is the easiest available target.

In my eyes, nothing Jan does is right. She doesn't clean well, she isn't fast enough and on top of all, it bothers me that she always looks so sad and unhappy.

One Day

I'm sitting in the living room with my baby and Jan comes in and hands the bottle of milk to me. She's been crying.

I ask her, "What's the matter?"

Jan says, "It's my birthday today!"

She holds her face and weeps out loud. I feel sorry for her, even though I think of birthdays as total nonsense. I get up and dress to go out. I bring Jan a cake and tell her to call her family to feel better. Jan seems to be calmer in the evening.

After that day ends, I am my old me toward her—full of criticism and demands.

After a Few Weeks

Jan hands a letter to me. The letter states that her father is very ill, and she has to travel home immediately. I realise that the letter is written by Jan and refuse to give her permission to travel home.

I'm very unhappy about her unhappiness, but think, "Shortly after my wedding, my father died. Within a year, I had my first baby. All my friends have gone from the city. My husband is at work all the time, and we have drifted apart. I have no social life. I am in a huge house, almost all alone, with my own piled-up sadness for different things. The last thing I want to deal with is a sad and homesick housemaid!"

Intercontinental

It's an ordinary morning, like any other morning. Jan and I prepare my baby and head to the hotel Intercontinental for a swim. My one-year-old loves playing in the baby pool, and while Jan is looking after him, I attend the aqua-aerobic session.

After about two hours, we are done and heading home. I park the car in our yard, Jan takes the baby stroller out from the trunk of the car and closes the trunk roughly. The banging sounds very loud in my ears, and, given the mid-day heat and my slight tiredness after swimming, I lose my temper completely and scream, "Why on earth did you bang the trunk of my car? You must be careful with our stuff. Why are you so careless?"

I yell continuously as Jan walks toward the front door to enter the house. I run after her, yelling, "I'm talking to you! Answer me!"

Jan doesn't say anything and walks toward the kitchen, crying. I follow her like a mad and barking dog, repeating, "Tell me! Why aren't you careful with our stuff? Tell me! Why on earth aren't you paying attention?"

Jan is standing by the sink in the kitchen with her back toward me and her head down, looking exhausted. Suddenly, she takes up a knife and holds it toward her stomach in a gesture that is clear, "If you don't stop talking, I'll use it!"

I freeze! I can't believe my eyes. I'm totally surprised by her reaction. I run fast toward her, almost snatch the knife from her hand and say in a gentler tone, "Why are you doing this?"

I try to calm her down, while shaking uncontrollably all over. I ask Jan to go and rest and take it easy in her room. I'm very afraid now, and think, "I didn't want Jan to harm herself. I just wanted her to say sorry and to say that she would be more careful next time."

Worried and still shaky, I keep going to Jan's room and checking on her. At one point, she runs out to the kitchen sink and gags. I'm very concerned and am desperately hoping that she'll be okay soon.

After a couple of hours, when my baby is fed, I put him down for his afternoon nap. Jan comes out from her room, and I help her eat something. Later on, when everything seems to be back to normal, at least on the surface, I light a cigarette, sit on the veranda and smoke, while thinking about what could have happened in the early hours of the afternoon in my home.

I'm happy that it seems that Jan is okay now.

I ask Jan to come and sit with me. I tell her, "I apologise for yelling at you earlier today. Please always be careful with our stuff!"

That Evening

Smoking another cigarette, I look into the dark night, asking myself, "Why aren't I nice to Jan? Why aren't I kind to her?"

I see that Jan is like me when I was little. I didn't say "stop" to anyone either and, throughout life, I didn't know how to set boundaries. I try to analyse it further, "Why am I like this toward her? I should be nice to her since I understand how it feels with all the injustice that happened to me when I was growing up. Why aren't I nice to her?"

At this stage, I am completely unaware of how one can get shaped and changed without even noticing, depending on what environment one finds oneself in. It's like getting the odour of bad-smelling surroundings and not being aware of it.

It seems I don't like weak people. I get upset when I see someone put herself down. I don't like it when someone plays small.

Jan reminds me of me, and it seems, with my way of being, unconsciously, I want to say these words to Jan and somehow to myself, "You silly and miserable girl! You let people walk all over you and make you feel little. Here you go! I will give you what you deserve. Just be quiet and take all the bad. No one is coming to your rescue anyway. You never complain to anyone. Oh! Damn you! I hate you. Why don't you say anything? Why don't you object?"

Yes, depending on the degree of our inner wound-related smallness, we can make others feel small in the same way. And 'miserable' and 'unhappy' can only create misery and unhappiness.

Break-up With My Childhood Friend

The phone rings. It is my childhood friend, and she is furious about some drama that has happened between our families. She sounds very upset and accusatory. I tell her that I can't deal with her and the dramas caused by others as I have enough on my own plate, dealing with my total loneliness in my new life.

I'm mourning the death of the happy and alive me. I have had enough of yelling and demeaning remarks in my home already, which I don't know how to deal with. I ask her, firmly, not to call me anymore if she wants to be like this!

One Year Later

We are moving to a smaller home today, and I'm wondering how to fit all our furniture in this tiny, new flat.

Jan is with me, and we are waiting for the furniture. I'm still always annoyed with her, even though she does all her work well.

Since it's a small flat and I still don't know where Jan is going to stay, I tell her, "Whenever you have nothing to do, just sit here until we know." I point to a chair near the door of the flat.

Jan stands up, crying, takes her bag and says, "Goodbye madam, I am going!"

I'm surprised, but I don't try to stop her. I think, somewhere inside, I'm happy to get rid of Jan. I roll my eyes, thinking, "Can't be bothered with you anymore! Can't be bothered to argue with you!"

I remember another incident from last month when she hit her head on the wall several times, crying and acting hysterically, just because I asked her not to give cookies to my boy without my permission.

I don't wish to be afraid of her mental reactions anymore.

I'm relieved she is gone.

Our Tiny Home

It's very convenient to have a tiny and compact place like this. I like this place, but I hate the balcony. It's full of the furniture from our old home. But this isn't the reason I don't like this balcony.

Every time I look at it—without knowing why—I am reminded of Jan's face, and at the same time, I get a flash of the memory of the knife, with her standing by the sink and gagging. So I don't like the sight of this balcony at all, not knowing completely how the balcony and Jan can be correlated in any way.

I am very happy that Jan left. She isn't missed here at all.

Back to Work

I go to work every morning. In the afternoons, I spend most of my time by the pool with my energetic twenty-month-old boy.

It's not my dream job, but it seems good enough for now. It gets me out of the house. I take my son to the nursery that I have started working at. It's cute to be the nurse on alert, in case someone scratches a knee or gets a bump in the head. My biggest intervention involves comforting the little ones with a magical plaster that actually works like a charm.

After two weeks in this place, I am discovering how everyone always seems to want a cuddle in this place.

"Please, please…can I have a cuddle? Can I have a cuddle?"

Although I'm very cuddly with my son, my spontaneous answer to the rest of them is usually, "Later, later. It's not the right time now. Wait a little."

~~~~

My husband is packing for a night flight. I'm feeling anxious, and I don't know why. I'm busy making tea for both of us. I sit next to him, still feeling shaky. He is rushing, working on his papers. I say, carefully, "I wish you didn't have to go."

Hesitantly, I continue, "Recently, I have been feeling down, sometimes anxious. Maybe I'm experiencing an early stage of depression."

He looks at me, looking *very* annoyed at being interrupted during his work, and says, "Please, I don't have time for your depression at all. Don't you see I'm always so busy!"

I sit there, watching him in disbelief, knowing that it hasn't been easy for me to ask for help. I have never done this before, since I've always been an 'I'll fix it by myself' type.

Disappointed, yet almost having expected this, unaware that everyone I meet in life is fighting a battle I don't know about, I just pull myself together and look away, but not toward the balcony. I don't want to worsen what I already feel.

I feel completely alone. I'm not allowed to feel anxious, not allowed to feel depressed, and on top of it, I'm supposed to pretend that everything is great.

Later that night, as he is leaving for the airport, I pretend that our conversation never happened, and he's doing the same.

I get into bed early, trying to avoid being anxious by not being awake.

Two Months Later

I eagerly look at the stick in my hand. Oh my God, I'm pregnant! I call him, and he is very happy. He surprises me with a massive bouquet of red roses.

~~~~

It's already been three months! I'm busy going to the nursery every day, even though I feel sick most of the time.

The Fifth Month

My tummy is growing bigger. So is my anxiety. I feel more anxious at night. Sleeping is like some form of medieval torture. I feel that I can't breathe and, therefore, I dread evenings and nights. I don't sleep well at night, and I wake up exhausted.

I feel frightened most of the time. I'm sensitive to noise and can't tolerate it when I hear people talking to me or even to each other.

I feel like being stuck in a tunnel, halfway in. The fear I'm experiencing is unfairly real, and all I want is just to run back to the beginning of the tunnel. I feel I can't continue in this dark tunnel anymore. It's scary—the scariest experience I've ever had.

I'm stuck in an impossible situation. I don't want to go on, and I can't go back.

~~~~

The days aren't passing, and my anxiety is getting worse. I've stopped eating after six in the evening. This does lessen the pressure over my chest. I feel less anxious on and off, but I still feel claustrophobic due to the whole pregnancy thing. I don't seem to be able to shake off this feeling of being fearful.

Two Weeks Before My Due Date

I'm so fed up that I beg my doctor to induce me. The doctor disagrees and tells me to go and wait for two more weeks.

Three Days Later

It's eight in the morning, and I'm up because I need to drink. I take a bit of watermelon instead, and I'm back in bed again. My two-year-old is playing in the living room with our nanny, Gallegoo. Her name is Kumari, but he calls her Gallegoo!

I roll on the bed to face my husband, and I suddenly feel that it's all wet under me. I think, "Oh my God! My water just broke! The baby is coming. Oh my God, my mom isn't here yet! She's coming after three days."

Eight at Night

My second baby is born. It's a boy. He is healthy and gorgeous. I'm the happiest person. I'm in seventh heaven. The telephone rings. It's my sister Tara. She is crying and says, "I've been so worried about you. I've been afraid that something might happen to you. You are there all alone! Mom isn't there yet. I wish I was there with you!"

I burst out crying too, a huge surge of mixed emotions surfacing all at once. I'm weeping, she is weeping, and my husband is just watching. My mother-in-law walks toward me and hugs me.

My husband asks, "Are you depressed?"

I don't know how to interpret his comment. It does not sound affectionate. It sounds more like he's making fun of and ridiculing me.

I think, "Maybe he doesn't want to show affection because his mother is in the room."

That Night

In the middle of the night, I wake up, extremely agitated. My husband is fast asleep on the couch. I don't want to disturb him. I don't wake him up.

Anxious All the Time

Very often during the week, I go to the grocery shop. I tell our nanny to hurry up and prepare the boys quickly, so we can all go together. I hurry up to get ready as if I must leave immediately, as if someone is chasing me out.

In the grocery shop, I put things I need in the trolley. I'm in a hurry. I'm telling the nanny to hurry up and get all the stuff we need, so we can get home as soon as possible.

Standing in the middle of the groceries with the cart full of things, I suddenly wonder, "Why did I buy all this?"

I realise I didn't really need any of this stuff. Then, I feel I have to get home as soon as possible. It's two in the afternoon. I think all the time, "I have to get home and get the food ready for dinner."

I get home and start preparing food, realising that everything I needed for this recipe was already in the refrigerator.

I hurry up, wanting to finish the food in one second. I tell the nanny, "Put everything in where it needs to go! Let's finish this and the food! I'm going to take the boys horseback riding! Let's hurry up!"

Within fifteen minutes, we are all sitting in the car again. I'm driving to the ranch, listening to music, thinking, "We'll finish this quickly, so I get home before he gets home! I still have to make salad."

Hungry

I seem to not feel full. Ever. I'm hungry all the time. I eat when I'm not hungry. I like to eat all the time. I eat when I'm nervous, which is almost all the time…

Forced to Look Back

In a dream, I see a house from a distance. I enter the dark house in the middle of the night, in the middle of nowhere.

While crying, I search inside every room of the house, upstairs and downstairs, desperately looking, thinking and screaming, "Where is my friend? Where is she? I need to find her!"

I wake up and notice that I've been dreaming. I'm extremely annoyed. It's almost as if I don't like to be awake. I worry, with my eyes full of tears, "Was my friend in that house? Why did I need to wake up? Why didn't I find her?"

I close my eyes, repeatedly thinking, "Sleep, sleep, sleep! Please, I want to go back to sleep again! I want to see her! I want to talk to her!"

Eventually, I slip into the dream state again. I see my childhood friend in a home with beautiful furniture. She seems happy and surrounded by her family, and I'm sitting next to her. In my dream, I'm thinking, "Thank God we are good with each other now. There is no trace of the conflict that caused us to not speak with each other for the last six years."

She has two babies, and she seems great with them.

The scene shifts in my dream. It seems that a while has passed, and now, she has only one baby. I wonder, "Where is your other baby?"

She replies without emotion, with cold, blank eyes, "My baby died!"

"What? What do you mean? No! No! No!"

Tears roll down my cheeks, and I'm weeping so loud that I feel a sharp pain in the deepest part of my bones.

I wake up again, finding myself holding my chest. I'm feeling an extreme sharp pain in my chest. I know I've been dreaming, but I think, "Oh my God, this felt so awfully real! Oh, my dear friend, where are you? I curse and damn the conflicts that came between us! What's happening in your life? I hope you are ok!"

I'm beside myself. I get up and walk toward my computer. I write a heartfelt email to her. It reads, "Friends are like pieces of a puzzle in one's life. If one piece is lost, that particular piece can *never* be replaced and the puzzle will never be whole again.

You were a big, crucial piece of the puzzle of my life, and I let you go a few years ago. As much as the reason for our fight seemed to be reasonable right at that time, the undeniable fact is that I truly miss you.

I don't know how to make it through all the 'downs' without you anymore. I'm not alone, but I'm so terribly lonely without you.

I hope you are doing well. I know for sure that I would have never been this down if you were still in my life. I hope my horrible nightmare is only a silly and meaningless dream.

I get it now—the saying that tells us that as we grow older, we need people in our life that knew us when we were younger.

I want you to know that I still remember that sad day I took the train to you—when I cried for eight hours non-stop. In the midst of those saddest hours of my life, I felt comforted because I knew I was coming to you.

I just want you to know that I wish you the best of best in life, from the bottom of my heart.

You know, I still smile each time I see two old ladies holding on to each other and walking past me. You used to say, 'Our future plan!' whenever you saw two old ladies walking together. We laughed so much about this.

I'm still counting on your prediction for our future!"

One Night

My three-year-old son is restless and can't sleep. I wake up easily. Most nights, when he sleeps restlessly, he comes to our bed. Tonight, he says, "Mom, I want milk!"

Holding him tight, I carry him to the refrigerator while hugging and kissing him. Pressing him to my chest and caressing his back affectionately, I whisper, "I love you, my love. I'll die for you…"

While waiting for the kettle to boil, I reminisce about that night many years ago when *I* was five, when I woke my mother up because something woke me up in the middle of the night and I was very scared. After she made me a cup of tea with crystal sugar, I had gone off to bed again.

I hand the bottle of milk to my son, holding him closer while kissing his forehead.

I tuck him in his bed and lay beside him until he falls asleep.

The Fall

I'm thirsty. It's three hours past midnight. I get up and slip my feet into my fluffy white slippers, my eyes barely open. I don't want to be awake, but I need to drink something badly. I think, "I'll remember to put a glass of water next to my bed tomorrow night."

The six-meter walk from my bed to the kitchen is interrupted by me hearing something.

"Don't look to your right! The balcony! Don't look at the balcony! You might want to throw yourself off. Don't look to your left! The kitchen knives are on the counter. You might want to slash the artery of your neck!"

Pearls of sweat cover my forehead. I freeze as I hear these rather strange voices,

"*You ugly witch!*
You know I like the water cold!
Weak!
Who cares how you look?"

And I see my life go by as if on rapidly changing slides:

Standing on one leg with my head down in first grade!
Mother slapping me in front of everyone!
Father spitting in my face!
My sister grinding her teeth!
My mother singing sadly!

My ex's ridiculing look, with his scathing remark, '*Don't think this will be waiting for you when you come home!*'.

My Greek boyfriend spitting on me, while looking cross.
My husband's annoyed look and remark, '*Please, I don't have*

time for your depression!'
My husband's ridicule, *'Are you depressed?'*

My sister's demanding look with her arms over her hips!
In the middle of the dark tunnel and frightened!
Afraid of his anger!
Anxious about all demands!
Jan's gagging!
Jan holding a knife toward her stomach.

I see myself throwing Jan's suitcase away, with all the gifts she had in it for her family.

I see myself standing on the edge of the rail of the balcony, ready to jump.
I see my husband holding our boys.
I see my children's sad eyes.

I can't take another step. I can't remember why I'm up and on the way to the kitchen. I am stricken by sheer fear and feeling paralyzed all over my body. At the same time, I feel like taking the knife and slitting my own throat. I blink rapidly, rubbing my eyes, hoping to wake up from this nightmare.

I turn my head carefully to the right to look at the big glass door of the balcony which is only seven meters away. I look to see where the voice comes from. I am still frozen and feel that I can't move a single muscle. My heart is beating fast, and I force myself back to my bed and crawl next to my husband.

I hug him as tight as I can, but the voices and all those rapidly changing pictures follow me to our bed.

I hear the vicious whispers over and over again, "Be very careful! You might want to throw yourself off the balcony! Just take the knife and slash your wrist!"

I shake uncontrollably. My husband notices that I'm shaking and wonders, "What's wrong?"

I answer, "I don't know why I'm suddenly so anxious!"

I don't dare to tell him what's going through my mind. The feeling of isolation adds to my anxiety.

He suggests, "Take a Xanax!"

I think, "Maybe I should open the balcony door and get some fresh air. Oh, no, I might jump! Oh, my God, what's going to happen to my children if I happen to kill myself?"

I close my eyes, trying to force myself to sleep. I keep seeing myself hanging by one arm from the railing of the balcony.

"I don't want to jump, what am I doing here? Why am I hanging here? I don't want to die!"

I hear again, "Come on, let go! Jump! There is no use! You are a horrible person. There is no hope for you. No one will miss you! You should die!"

I open my eyes. I get up. I can't stand still. I walk to the living room again, shaking. I'm hugging my stomach and gasping for air. My heart is still racing, I'm terrified of the thought that I actually might throw myself off the balcony.

Again, I think, "What will happen to my boys? Who is going to take care of them? What if I do something to them? Oh my God! This isn't happening. I don't want to feel like this."

I hear the same soundless voice I once heard on the veranda in LA, "Prostrate yourself! You need to get down on your knees. Prostrate yourself!"

I'm helpless and without knowing why, I'm on my knees, bending forward. I put my forehead on the bare ground and start weeping. I still see all the rapidly changing pictures and hear the mind-scratching noises in my head.

After ten minutes on the ground, shedding tears, I feel a sudden relief. I'm ok, suddenly. Exhausted, yet lightened, I get up, walk to the kitchen, get water and then walk to my bed.

I fall asleep immediately!

Full Cup

I have woken up feeling lighter than last night. The prostration helped. I slept like a trouble-free baby. I am happy.

A Week Later

The anxiousness is back. Deeper, darker than before. It looks like it is here to stay longer this time.

~~~~

My babies are in the nursery, and I feel less anxious as I feel they are in better hands than my own. I keep having disturbing thoughts, "Maybe you will hurt your children like that woman you saw in the news, who drowned her two children in the pool."

I feel very scared when I hear this. I know it's not me because I know that I love my children, but this voice in my head worries me. I feel paralyzed by it, and as a result, I feel afraid of being alone with my boys.

One evening, I gather my courage, and I tell my husband about my bothersome thoughts. He just laughs and brushes off what I tell him, "Ah, you are not capable of doing such a thing! You'll never harm our boys!"

As kind and reassuring as that sounds, it's not taking away the fear and the anxiety that I feel every time these voices pop up.

I feel worse when it's noisy around me. Sometimes I just go

to my bedroom and lock the door while the nanny is watching them. The worst of the worse is how I feel when our nanny has the day off.

I feel that I'm walking on the thinnest ice. I take all my steps carefully. I force myself to stay calm. I'm afraid of myself, and I'm afraid of my own thoughts, and worst of all, I can't tell anyone.

A Few Weeks Pass

I'm not expecting anything, but still no letter from my childhood friend. What I really want to believe is that the letter has been lost or something. I think, "It's ok! In my mind I will continue talking to you!"

Swan Lady

God is good. When one door closes, another one opens.

I'm in the pool, and as I gaze at the blue water, while my three-year-old is swimming, my eyes catch a mother and a daughter walking by the pool. The mother seems to be a lady around her mid-thirties. She walks elegantly while holding her daughter's hand. The immediate thought that pops up in my head when I see her is, 'Swan'! She is like an elegant swan! She walks so beautifully.

I think, "Why aren't I elegant like her?"

While I'm swimming, she comes into the water, swims toward me and starts talking to me. She seems very kind. I like her immediately. I'm ok letting her be my friend.

Venice Again

Yippie! Finally, after so many years, I am going to have a chance be in Venice again.

I think, "This time I'm going to do what I couldn't do last time. I'm going to live it and feel alive in this city. I'm going to enjoy the natural beauty of this magical floating city. I'm going to let the rays of the sun take me with them to the romantic corners of aliveness, where I can fly."

It is a rainy day, and we have to be in Milan tonight for a company retreat.

On the way to Venice, we get into a fight.

Not in the greatest mood after our fight, we walk around in the city of Venice.

I think sadly about the promise I made to myself years ago, "One day, I'll come back here again with someone I love."

We reach the train station just in time to hop in. I am left with the feeling of unfinished business again! I feel an empty place in me that is still yearning to fill up. The train starts rolling, and the green trees and houses planted in water pass by my eyes like a movie on high speed.

Completely unaware of the preciousness and the fleeting nature of each moment, I can't shake off and let go of the effect of a trivial fight on my mind, and therefore, I think remorsefully, "It didn't happen this time either! Maybe next time! Or maybe I should just give up on Venice and chasing after romance in this city."

Day Off

My mother-in-law is taking care of my boys, so I can just relax and take care of myself. I am very happy that I can simply go away for one day and just relax!

In the spa, I ask for a full body massage. It feels wonderful and relaxing. Ten minutes into the massage, I'm feeling ice-cold all over my body, and a huge surge of anger comes upon me. I'm so cold and so mad that I feel, for one instant, that I want to kill the girl who is massaging me, right there at that moment.

Frightened by my own disturbing thoughts, I think I'm going mad, and now realise that I truly need help.

Visit to the Doctor

"Maybe my hormones are not balanced, and maybe I should go and see a gynaecologist to give me a pill or something to fix it."

So I decide to go to the hospital.

While feeling very agitated, I tell the doctor, who is a woman, "I'm anxious all the time. I need your help!"

She asks me, "Why do you think you are anxious?"

I cry, "I'm very afraid that I might hurt my children. I have stupid thoughts most times."

She looks at me for a second, and then she continues writing the prescription as if she didn't hear what I told her.

Housemaid Number 7

Almas means 'diamond' in Farsi, and it's the name of my seventh housemaid. She is a dark-skinned Ethiopian woman in her thirties. She is kind, caring, sweet and protective and, overall, with good vibes. Sometimes, because of my hyper-sensitivity to noise, I would turn into a raging and screaming maniac.

During the one month that she stays with us, there are many sweet incidents, some of which make me laugh. One day, I yell at the boys, because I do not want them to bug each other so much and not make so much noise, so 'I' can remain calm and sane.

She throws herself on my children, trying to protect them from my nervousness and screaming, with a big smile on her face.

Unfortunately, she only stays with us for a month, but I will always remember her as our sweet diamond. She was a rare kind in her kindness...

Dinner Invitation

I'm invited to dinner at my swan lady's house. My whole family is here, but I still feel anxious. I seem not to be able to shake off this feeling of anxiousness, these butterflies in the stomach, no matter where I am and what I do.

The boys are playing with my friend's daughter. Everyone is busy eating the delicious dinner, and I'm still wrestling with my anxiety. After dinner, swan lady gives me that look which says, "tell me what's going on,' and I get the feeling that I have no choice but to tell my friend what's going on.

"I really don't feel well. I don't know how to describe how badly I feel. I just know that I'm really feeling bad."

A friend of swan lady is also there. She immediately responds as if she already knows all about me not feeling so good. She says, "I've heard about some classes. You could search about them online. They claim to be 'knowing yourselves' classes, something called Erfane Halghe (Interuniversal mysticism). Maybe these could help you? I've heard people have noticed great results. They will help you discharge all the bad stuff inside."

I'm not sure if I understand what she means, but I respond, "Why not! I'll try anything."

The Next Day

I search for the course online, read about it and don't understand anything, so I give up reading further about the course.

I make an appointment for a session of something called EFT, Emotional Freedom Technique, which I read about in a magazine.

EFT—First Session

I need something to fix me and fix me quickly, although I don't know what to expect at all. I think, "I can't possibly feel any worse than I already feel now. I'll try anything. I need to get out of this mess as soon as possible!"

I'm sitting on a chair in a little room opposite a lady who starts tapping on the various areas of my body—the top of my head, my forehead, between my eyebrows, under my nose, on my chin to the side of the head, on my wrists, on my ankles and on my knees. She asks, "Tell me what comes up as I tap."

With my eyes closed, I feel surprised when I hear myself saying, "I had to break contact with my sister!"

She asks gently, "Tell me about it."

I continue, "After I got married and had my children, it all became too much for me. The pressure of hosting others was just like pure torture, since I was already under maximum amount of pressure. I had to cut contact as the demands from everyone and the zero support were way too much for me!"

She asks, "What else? Do you see anything as I tap?"

I say, "I'm ten years old, playing pull and push with my friends. Their mother comes to me and says, 'Be careful! You might hurt my children.'

And the mother pulls one of her daughters away from me."

She asks, "What else?"

I feel and look sad. I want to cry again. I'm not sure, but I say, "The other day, my husband was holding me from behind in bed. It reminded me of the time during my cousin's engagement and the rubbing in the middle of the night. I felt sick. I felt cold. I didn't want to be reminded of this memory. In that moment, without knowing why, I just wanted to die."

As I say this, I feel that I'm suffocating, I gasp for air. I hold the EFT lady's hand.

"Oh my God, I can't breathe!"

I stand up, and I hear a woman's voice screaming inside me, "Open the window and jump out! You have to get air. Do it! If you jump out, you will get air. I did that once. Don't worry, just do it! Just throw yourself out!"

I hear something in my thoughts instructing me, compelling me, urging me, and I feel like I *must* listen, despite knowing about the craziness of what I hear.

I scream, "No! Oh my God! Oh my god!"

Gasping for air, I walk toward the window. The EFT lady

holds me and says, "Don't worry! Sit down! I know how to handle this! Sit down! Don't worry!"

I sit down. Her assurance calms me down. I take a few guided deep breaths, and I'm better immediately.

The tapping continues, and I speak about the sadness that I feel about my choice-less break up with my older sister. This time, I do it without gasping for air.

My forty-five-minute session is done, and I go home. All I think about is my bed. I feel that I can stay asleep forever.

In the Evening

I wake up after sleeping for three hours. I feel light. I do my tapping as the EFT lady showed me. I'm very happy about this learned technique.

My babies are settled in their bed. I go to the balcony, light a cigarette, and, while looking at the sea, I think about my older sister again, "I know she was very helpful and good for many years, but with me just getting married and having a new baby, having non-supportive guests felt like a nightmare. I needed my sisters as support and as a source of comfort, but everyone just wanted to come and visit and be guests, while I was running around and arranging things. In the end, I was at a point where I announced to everyone that I needed to be alone with my new life and my new problems.

"I needed to know how to handle my troubles with my husband who treated me like a badly-behaved employee. I needed to know how to handle my housemaid. I had to deal with the mean 'Me', whom I didn't like at all, but still let her run the show with those weaker than me.

"In that already fully-crowded war zone and battlefield, there was no place for anyone else, unless that person was supportive and loving. Unfortunately, no one fit that description then."

I look at the calm sea and, feeling extremely comforted by these explanations to myself and without feeling guilty for being selfish, I whisper, "I needed friends. I needed true sisters, but the ones I had added to my burdens, rather than releasing pressure.

"I needed to ask for help, but didn't see anybody volunteering. I was drowning. I needed to save myself first. I needed to find ways to know how to survive my new life first."

Stirred Up

I feel so much better these days. I do my tapping routinely, going to the gym with my new friend.

Swan lady tells me, while we are walking on treadmills in the gym, "Oh, by the way, do you remember that 'knowing yourself class' my friend was talking to you about? I've found someone in this city, near to our home who is teaching it. Let's do that. What do you think?"

I think that I feel excellent now, with the tapping and all, but since it is something to do with my friend, I agree, not knowing what's waiting on this road that I have just been invited to walk on.

~~~~

On the way back from the gym after taking a shower, I feel a choking sensation in my throat. I want to run away and get out of there as soon as possible. I can't tolerate the small talk of folks in the gym. I feel drained, and I just want to go home and lock myself in my bedroom and fall asleep.

The swan lady is looking at me, surprised, with fearful eyes.

She half screams, "What's that? Why is your upper lip swollen like that? And the side of your throat has a huge bump. When we exercised, you didn't look like this!"

I hurry to the mirror and look at my face. I notice that I look like I've been beaten up badly. I, too, notice a big and visible bruise on my right cheek. Although all this looks terrifyingly bad, it doesn't bother me as much as the choking sensation in my throat and the hyper-sensitivity to everybody talking.

We dress and walk out toward the parking lot. I'm thoughtful, and so is my friend who is looking at me with worried and terrified eyes.

By the time we reach our cars, the swollenness and the bruise are completely gone.

If only it was possible to see what we accumulate inside and attract around us every single time we are in a negative state of mind.

Already Invited

I go home and go straight to bed. I dream of being in a classroom and the founder of the 'knowing yourself' classes, Dr Mohammad Ali Taheri, is there and conducting the class.

He holds up a paper to show me something that is written on it. He says, pointing to the paper, "Here is your signature, and here is mine."

The First Day of Class

I feel excited going to the first day of my 'knowing yourself' meeting. I don't have any idea what it's about, but I'm very eager to find out, especially after my encounter with the founder of Interuniversal Mysticism in my dream.

I tell the swan lady, "What does 'knowing yourself' mean anyway? Of course, we all know ourselves, don't we? I'm going because you are going. How bad could it be? Worst case scenario, we giggle a lot and have a good time as we always do when we are together."

It is four hours now that we've been sitting here and listening to our teacher in the 'knowing yourself' class. She is talking about things I've never heard before.

We are instructed to close our eyes and merge into something that is called 'connection'.

Although for four hours, I have not understood even one single word, I do as I am instructed.

"Connection is the magic word!"

As we walk out of the teacher's house, I can only think about one word that's been mentioned repeatedly—a word which I have never heard before and don't understand—'Consciousness'.

Imagine if all 'we' are is limited to the knowing of our names and gender and people we think we are related to. What a waste of creation and purpose that would be compared with everything that truly is…

And imagine if all 'we' are would be so limited that even a five-year-old would be able to condemn the creator of all for it.

Normal

Usually, I wake up after nine hours of sleeping at night and still feel very tired. I feel tired all the time, and I wish I wasn't. I miss the never-tired me that I used to be.

I don't know why it's like this now. Sometimes, during the day, I feel exhausted, but I can't allow myself to fall asleep. It is as if something is telling me, "You need to be careful! You need to be awake in case something is about to happen, so you can prevent it. Keep awake!"

~~~

Night has fallen, and I can't sleep, so I think, "Let me try this! Let me close my eyes and see what will be."

I close my eyes, say 'connection to the link of Faradarmani,' and within a few seconds, I'm in the deepest sleep.

I see myself yelling at someone, "I hate it. I hate it. I hate it. I hate you and that you are trying to make me do this!"

She calmly says, "I understand!"

"No! You don't! Every time you want me to tell you what happened, I really get uncomfortable. I really want to jump and grab your neck and strangle you! Do you understand? I wish you were dead. I don't know why I feel this way. I just know I don't want to answer your questions.

Or I would like to give you those rosy answers, like the perfect answers people give each other when they meet.

'Hi, how are you? Oh, yes, I'm great!' these types of answers."

She says, "So, why don't you tell me the true version of how you are? Your heart's story! The story that only you know every detail of. After all, you are here to do this, right?"

I think for a moment, look at this woman who looks so familiar, with her kind and motherly eyes, and say, "I don't know why I'm here. I don't even know who you are! I don't like to be pushed. I hate being forced into doing this, and I don't like this at all!"

"What? What is it that you don't like?"

I cry, "I hate my life story. I really don't like my story. That's why I don't like to admit it to you, to me, or to anyone else, for that matter. I hate myself, and I hate my name. Most times I just want to die!"

A memory from a few years ago shows up.

I'm in my psychology class during my junior nursing program. My teacher is asking everyone to paint whatever comes to mind.

It's time for the teacher to evaluate my painting. Smiling, he says, "What a nice and colourful layer of frames you have done for your painting! Your whole painting is layers of colourful frames!"

A twenty-year-old me asks, with a smile, "What does it mean? It's beautiful, right?"

My teacher answers, "It means you hide everything within all these pretty colourful frames. You don't show or tell anything to anyone!"

While looking at her, tears roll down my cheeks. I try very hard to stop them, but it's already too late.

I hear a flute playing in the background, leaving me no choice but to talk to this marvellous-looking lady, dressed like an angel, in a long white dress.

I say, "I thought things would be different. I thought I would be happy after I got married this time, since this time I did it for all the right reasons, for love. But I feel afraid most of the time. I'm afraid of doing something wrong, and as hard as I try not to,

I still hear my husband somehow finding fault with everything I do. It seems, in his eyes, I don't talk well and I don't look good.

"It was very unfortunate that my dad died right after our wedding and threw me in a ditch of sadness I wasn't prepared for yet. And right after that, I got pregnant. It all was happening too soon, too fast.

"I stopped working, stayed at home and did everything that I had to do to be a good wife. I really tried, but something wasn't right, right from the start.

"Things were different when we were dating. We were always out dancing with friends. Sometimes I would get to the dancing place earlier or later, and no matter what the case—my friends told me that as soon as he would arrive, the first thing he would ask would be, 'Where is Rebecca?'

"Actually, he still does it, but mostly just to point out what's not right, or what mistake I have made, and how I can fix it and make sure it doesn't happen again.

"So when he calls out my name now, I feel afraid, because I feel he wants to say something unkind again.

"I was so bombarded with criticism and so filled with the unbearable odour of the toxic environment I lived in, that I needed to spill the load onto something, or someone, else. And Jan perfectly fit the cheese 'role' in this 'cat over mouse and mouse over cheese' story.

"Nothing that poor girl ever did was right in my eyes, although she was waking up early in the morning and working all day in our home that was the size of a mini palace.

"So the game went like this. I put her down, and my husband put me down, and the more I was nasty to her, the nastier my husband was to me.

"Or perhaps it was vice versa."

I take a brief moment, smile bitterly, and continue, "It's funny! He never saw me being nasty to her. How was this possible?

"After my first boy was born, I wanted to work out and get back in shape like before. Sometimes he would say—in a ridiculing tone—to our barely six-month-old baby, '*Mom is trying to lose weight, so she can find someone else!*'

"And when I persisted with my workout, sometimes he would say, '*Who cares what you look like?*'

"As sad, uncomfortable and puzzled as I was every time, I never asked him why he was saying all those hurtful things to me.

"Why was he treating me like an unwanted guest?

"I was too afraid of hearing the truth that was already written all over his remarks. What made me sad then, and does even now, was not knowing for sure why he was doing this.

"I was doing *everything* that I was supposed to do. The more I tried, it seemed to me, the lesser he saw and the nastier he got.

"To please him was like trying to fill an unfillable hole.

"I seem totally unaware of this Persian proverb that says, "When the niceness exceeds a certain limit, the fool gets the wrong idea."

"I don't seem to know that being too 'nice' can be a dangerous thing in the world we are living in.

"I don't seem to have the slightest idea that no one—not even I—can ever fill someone else's unfillable hole within."

I continue.

"One time, my old roommate, from my working days, Luis, came to visit us, and for old time's sake, all of us decided to go out, to one of those clubs that we used to go out to and dance at. Before we left home, he came to me and showered me with these exact words,

"When we are out in the club, I won't stand next to you!"

I stood there, stunned, speechless, not knowing where all these hostilities came from.

Even though I knew this was him being himself, as usual, this time I answered back, perhaps because I felt safe having my friend there.

I dared to say, "Actually, that would be very good! I don't want you to stand next to me either. It's never fun when you are around, anyway!"

I think out loud, to myself more than to the lady, "When people get married, all the family members are eager to gather, to celebrate, to support, but also, somehow, to show the newcomer in the family that, *hey, if you think you can do whatever here, you are going to deal with us!*

"That's why this picture isn't right. I am on my own, as usual, all over again. There is no family member or friend to stand up for me in case the fool gets the wrong idea. And as sad as it is to admit, it seems most people get the wrong idea in a situation like this, including me.

"Very little do I know, at this stage, that one must learn how to stand up for oneself and not rely on others' protection and rescue all the time.

"We went out that night. He never left our—my—side for a moment. Maybe he just needed me to stand up and answer him back the way I did.

"But, after that night, nothing changed. In fact, it only kept getting worse."

I see that the angel-like lady is still listening, so I continue, On another occasion, our baby's eye was slightly infected, and it was very clear that he needed some eye drops. I looked at him, and wondered if we should go and buy the eye drops. What I saw in his eyes could be described as him screaming, '*You* are the mom. Go and buy it yourself! We have a nanny to look after him! I'm already doing enough. I'm working every day. This is *your* job. Not mine!'

"Like the good girl that I knew very well how to be, I didn't argue. I didn't push him. I got up, dressed and went out and bought the eye drops. I kept thinking, 'It's not a big deal. This isn't difficult! Of course, I can also do this by myself!'

"But only I know what I saw in his eyes, at that moment. I was trying to pretend that I didn't get what I saw—the total lack of unity, and an absolute lack of love."

I continue thinking, "Fair enough! He is working and earning money, but please, someone tell me, what has happened to the guy who would look only for me when he entered a party? The guy who wanted to marry me? The guy who I agreed to marry? What happened to that guy? Why am I at square one all over again? Why am I dressed in that good-girl outfit again? The good girl that nobody saw, the good girl that everybody did and said whatever they felt like to?

"Why? WHY?"

I find myself eye to eye with the angel-like lady again.

"Do you now see why I don't like my story? See why it makes me hate me? I don't like myself in it. I don't like to be the good girl, but in some ways, I am that girl. Whoever I come across, whoever I'm with, I end up in the same ditch again.

I don't like myself. This is my problem. I don't like myself, and I don't like my story at all.

I wish I would die soon. I wish I knew how to be, so that others would be nice to me."

I cover my face with my hands, weeping. The angel-like lady

in the white dress looks at me compassionately, like a kind mother.

I go on, "I want to know how to like myself. I want to look in the mirror and see that I'm beautiful. I *don't* want to hear, 'weak,' and 'who cares what you look like?' I want to be free from this constant feeling of doing something wrong all the time."

She asks, "Who are *you*? Who is the one who is the weak and the ugly one?"

I'm about to answer, but I stop instead. Suddenly, I don't know what's happening. My mind is blank. I have that feeling again—I don't know who I am. I don't know *where* I am.

I see a flash in which I am in a hospital and taking care of someone. That someone is in bed, and I'm the nurse. When I look closer, I see myself on the bed, looking very ill.

I see the angel-like lady in front of me, and suddenly, I'm back from that peculiar instant that I had seemed to disappear completely in. I say, "Oh, excuse me! What did you just ask me? Ask me again please!"

The angel-like lady says smilingly, "Who are you? Who is the one who is weak? Who is the ugly one?"

"Who am I? I'm Rebecca of course!"

"Who is Rebecca? What does 'I'm Rebecca' mean? Could you specify?"

I continue, "I'm a woman, mother of my two boys. I'm unhappy about my looks, I'm unhappy about everything. I'm weak, I hate myself, I hate my life. That's who I am. Is this what you wanted me to say? Are you happy now?"

The lady responds calmly, "Are you sure that's who you are? Are you *absolutely* sure about that?"

I start to weep again, and say, "Believe me, I want to feel different. I really want to feel good. I want to feel cute in my own eyes and also in other people's eyes. Mostly in other people's eyes, actually. If others think I'm cute, that's good enough!"

I sniff in-between my weeping, and then continue again, "I like to feel loved, and I want to love myself. How can I get that? How can I become that?"

Now, I see a tall middle-aged guy, with long hair, in a long white dress, walking toward me. He takes my hand, walks me toward a forest. Still weeping, I follow him helplessly.

Unlike my usual self, I feel safe with this guy. I don't have that normal crumbling sensation I have when I'm around men. We reach a fireplace. It's cold. It's the middle of the night now. I sit down by the fire, looking at the flames, wrapped in a thick blanket.

I feel like it's only the blanket, the fire and me with my tears. I hear the guitar. He walks toward me while I'm still crying, my head resting over my hugged knees. He plays the guitar and sings,

Hey you! The beautiful one who loves to be in love
You, who is the life of the passing minutes,
You, with tulips clipped on your hair

He comes closer to me, sits behind me, hugs me and continues playing the guitar and singing. I hold on to my knees. The left side of my face is resting on my knees, looking at the fire. I lift my head and hold it against his right shoulder while he embraces me from behind.

I shed tears, weeping, holding my face with one hand, hiding my face in the front part of his shoulder.

I think, "I have tried endlessly my entire life to make others think that I'm smart, cute and good. I have begged endlessly for other people's love and approval. And now I really feel that I don't want anyone anymore."

I realise that I've been living in a castle of false hope, chasing some white rabbit all along. I remember all the countless times I fell in love with guys, hoping to feel beautiful through their opinion about me, through their eyes.

Right at this moment, as this man is singing, I really know that's not possible, and even if I'm still crying, I'm ok with this bittersweet knowing. The tears are coming out like a river of emotions for all my efforts, for all my wasted energies.

He continues to sing, while still holding me:

Hey you, the nice smelling flower in the middle of the night
The flower of aliveness...
Hey you, whose eyes are shining like the eyes of a ghazal,
My heart is the tulip that is madly in love with you.
Hey you, the softest of all,
Please don't break the unopened flower of my heart,
I have fallen in love with you...
Why did you forget about me?
Tell me, to the one who is madly in love with you,
Why am I too much for you?
Hey you, the sound of the guitar,
Hey you, the heart on the wall,
If you don't hold my hands, then it will be goodbye,
Goodbye...

I think, "I really want to know what to do. Where shall I go from here? If I'm not to find love elsewhere, what am I going to do then? How shall I get that feeling of serenity? How? Where shall I start?"

I weep on his shoulder as he carries on with the song, playing the guitar with indescribable kindness in his eyes.

Your heart is the emotional Jasmine,
Hey you, my adorable flower,

Hey you, the flower of all flowers,
Until my last pulse, I'll be composing lyrics for you,
I will compose songs for you...
You are my song and my musical instrument,
I want to make a cage for you with this sound.

I wake up.

Recreating

We are in a shopping mall. My children are nagging me, my husband is nagging me.

"Hurry up! Hurry up! "

My memory pulls me back to our trip to Mashhad many years ago, when I was little. It was a trip full of stress and unrest and upsetting moments. It was past lunchtime, and dad was upset and wanted to hurry. He wanted us to hurry.

"What does it mean to feel peace? Those people who are calm and together, who don't have butterflies in their stomach, what kind of life do they have?"

I wonder...

We get home from the mall, and, exhausted by all the noise and unrest, I sit in the living room. I look through the big windows that are facing our garden which is full of trees that are almost covering the short wall. The sun is shining, and I'm mesmerised by these beautiful leaves of our trees.

They are moving gently, harmoniously.

Behind the trees and behind the wall that separates our villa from the outside, I can see people walking past and hear the murmuring sound of their quiet conversations.

I've seen this somewhere! Where have I seen it? My auntie's

house in the middle of the forest?

I hear my name being called, and I walk upstairs to see what my boys want. I find the boys deeply engaged with their games. They say they haven't called me at all. I walk out of their room and am on the way down, toward my beautiful living room scene.

I hear a whisper, a soundless sound, together with a sharp pain in my throat and stomach which is hard to ignore,

"Rebecca! Wake up! Rebecca!"

I hear an eager voice calling me from far away and, yet, it feels like it's right here, and, at the same time, everywhere. I'm confused, and think, "Am I really hearing this? Or is this, too, part of my vivid imagination?"

It feels like a woman desperately and eagerly calling my name from the bottom of a well.

"Rebecca!"

"Rebecca!"

I try to ignore what I hear, but I do stop for a moment as I'm walking down the stairs. Now I feel as if someone in the street is calling my name and asking for help. I stand still, thinking, "What's going on?"

I enter the kitchen and prepare an omelette with cheese and dill for myself, and while carrying the tray up, for a moment I take a bite as the omelette looks irresistible.

I hear again, "Rebecca! Wake up! Open your eyes!"

Suddenly, I'm filled with a huge feeling of shame, a volcano of boiling anger rising from somewhere deep within my stomach.

With clenched teeth, I scream.

I'm barefoot in a yard, green trees everywhere, feeling the uneven muddy ground under my feet. I'm still screaming but not from the bottom of my lungs. It's coming from the tips of my toes, all the way through my body and out from my mouth.

The sharp pain in the back of my throat isn't stopping me from screaming because I feel I still haven't reached the point where the bottom of that scream is hiding.

No, I haven't reached it yet.

I want to stop, because of the pain in my throat and the exhaustion, but somehow, I'm not able to.

Somehow, I feel like it's not me who's doing the screaming. It's happening to me on its own and, simultaneously, a river of uncontrolled tears is rolling down my cheeks.

I lay on wet mud, screaming and weeping.

A powerful voice commands me,

"Scream!

"There were hundreds of occasions when you should've screamed! You allowed your new, teenaged, blossoming body to be fiddled by selfish hands.

"Scream!

"On so many occasions you let yourself be belittled and pushed around. So many times, you witnessed unfairness, and you didn't stand up for yourself. You deserved to be encouraged, and no one offered it! You didn't dare to ask for what was your basic right!

"You were off lists of invitations and you noticed, but you always found a phony excuse for their unfairness."

"Oh, my God, I feel like I'm choking."

I continue hearing, "You *should* have screamed when your older sister forbade you from playing with your few friends when you were only ten years old, but instead, you just obeyed.

"You should have screamed when you saw the demeaning and ridiculing look on your sister's face when she heard that your mom bought you a drink in that market.

"You didn't scream then, so scream them off now!

"You cared too much about others opinions, cared too much about others' demeanour and their behaviour. You let others run the show even though you hated every single second of it.

"Scream!

"You let yourself be little, so others could remain big and inflated."

"SCREAM!"

I'm still on the ground, screaming, crying and thinking, "Oh, my God! I'm *so* angry. I want to hit the ground with my fist, so the earth itself breaks in half!

"Why did she look at me and roll her eyes like that? Shouldn't I ask for a drink if I feel like having one? What did my sister have to do with me asking for a drink anyway? Why did it bother me how she looked at me? Why did my mom tell her that she bought me a drink? Why did her sour look bother me? It was none of her business. It shouldn't bother me but it did!"

I mumble, shaking my head, "Yes, I held it all inside for too long, so many thousands of times."

I am still laying on the ground, still all muddy. I hear, "You must take the train!"

I look around and think, "There are no trains around here, but I wish there were because I really feel that I need to go away from here."

I'm afraid of what I'm seeing! My suitcases are packed, and I'm dressed to go away.

"I need to be free. I need to have another life. I can't bear this feeling of being unhappy anymore."

I see myself waiting for a taxi to come and take me away. I don't know where, just away from here!

"I can't do this anymore. I don't think I can bear one more demeaning remark. I can't bear to be ignored, and I can't bear one more look filled with ridicule. I don't think I can tolerate one more criticism. I don't want it.

"I only know that I have become so many things during all these years—nice, kind, aggressive, good, bossy, too little, too much, too sad, too happy, too angry with me, too angry with others, suicidal, depressed, delusional.

"I only know that I will choke if I stay one more second. I need to go away, so I can think clearly.

"I don't want *anything*. I just want to be free. I just want to be by myself so I can find answers. I need to find that happy Rebecca again. The one everyone called sunshine, the happy contagious soul, the one with positive energy, the one that never got tired.

"What happened to me? I don't know this Rebecca. I feel broken, and I don't want to be broken anymore."

I see my childhood friend's face in my mind, smiling at me, and I think, "Oh, I miss you, my friend. Where are you? I wish you were here. I wish I could take the train to you and you would hide me in your home, forever."

I open my eyes, looking up at the sky, holding the back of my neck with both my hands, sobbing, thinking, "Oh God, or whatever! You say you are as near to us as the artery of our neck. Tell me what to do? Show me the way! I want to go away for good. I need to take care of myself. I will die here if I don't go!"

I see my head—all my life—on other's shoulders. I see the poor and small Rebecca. I see the 'little me star' clearly this time. I don't like this 'little,' 'small' person at all.

"Should I go to those shoulders? Shall I speak to my friend? No! I have done this *too* many times in my life. I can *not* do this anymore. Where shall I go now? Where is that damn train?"

Even in this dream-like state, my despair is greater than my sadness. I see myself with my suitcases, and the taxi is there, ready to take me. I'm shivering as I see the faces of my children. My body suddenly feels ice-cold. I'm about to step into the taxi, but my legs are paralyzed. I can't walk.

I hear that deep voice again, "To leave and run isn't what you need! Running won't get you anywhere! You know very well how to cut and how to run. This time, you need to do something else!"

I start crying, knowing the truth about what I hear.

I decide to stay.

Even in my dream, I go back inside.

Now I find myself sitting on the couch in my living room.

No more whispers, no more voices, no more taxis, no more nothing.

I feel completely empty and numb, and yet, I feel ok!

It's Friday

Almost like any other Friday, we have visitors in our home. I am by the pool, enjoying the ordered food, watching the children play and all. It's been a great, full day of having people around, but now that the evening is here, it would be nice to have some peace and quiet. It would be nice to put my head on my husband's lap and just chill in front of the television. I feel restless, seeing my living room still full of visitors waiting for their never-arriving ride.

I really feel like screaming as this is not an unusual occurrence. My privacy is violated, and I find myself, as if, in the middle of a busy and noisy 'fruit market' where intimacy is at level zero. I find myself choking up again…

To prevent myself from losing it totally in front of our visitors, I close my eyes and reside in the "connection." Finally, after one agonising hour of waiting, the ride for my visitors is here, and everyone is finally gone.

I sit next to my husband and lay my head on his lap. I am tearful. I lift my head, look at him and say, "I feel so sad that we never have our cosy, private time, just us and our boys."

He looks at me and has a bitter smile, as if, somehow, he is agreeing with me. I'm still in the grip of the turmoil within.

"Why is it like this? When is my time? Until when do I have to put others' comfort first?"

We go upstairs to the bedroom and lay on the bed. I still have the choking sensation. I'm crying quietly and hope that he doesn't notice. He does, from my sniffing. He rolls toward me, holds me and asks me, "What's wrong?"

Not knowing where to start and tell him about all the hurt that is bubbling up to the surface, I continue to cry, sniff and cry. I have to go to the bathroom and blow my nose because I feel I can't breathe. I really want to stop crying so I can go to bed and try not to think about all the sad feelings, but in less than one minute, I weep again, thinking, "When is my time then?"

For an hour, I cry non-stop, and in-between, I go to the bathroom and blow my nose and come back to bed and cry again. On my last trip to the bathroom, I look in the mirror. My eyes and nose are so swollen that I don't recognise my face in the mirror.

Back to bed and after lots of tosses and turns, I eventually fall asleep.

I hear, "Pay attention to the dance! Pay attention!"

"What dance?"

"You are sleeping, your husband is sleeping, and everything's exactly the way it should be!"

I see a woman in the distance, holding a pickaxe, digging the ground!

~~~~

In the morning, he leaves for work after he kisses me goodbye. He hasn't asked me what was wrong with me last night, and I haven't told him what caused my breakdown. But I have woken up today, knowing that I don't want to play this game anymore.

I definitely want more. I want my right.

~~~~

Like any other day, I get ready and start the day by taking the boys to school. On the way to school, as I drive, I remember my encounter with myself. I still feel strange remembering all the turmoil that came rushing at me in one go.

While driving, I try to ignore the sensation of a vacuum in my head. I hear again, "Weak!

"Ugly!

"Who cares how you look!

"Just shut up!

"No one cares about your opinion!

"Hurry up! You're late!"

At the same time, I hear Dr Taheri's voice mentioning a verse from the holy book, the Quran, "Die before dying."

I don't understand it.

I hear, "You need to die! You need to die before dying! You are a sinner, Rebecca!"

I continue driving in this vacuum-like state, continue to see myself throughout my life—between my mom and dad when they were having a heated argument, fearing that it might escalate into something physical, even if that never happened. I see my right knee getting locked from all the stress I was dealing with. It goes on.

My head feels like a giant, pulsing ball. I can barely keep my eyes open. I see the road as if I'm looking through a pair of binoculars. Everything seems to be so strangely formed.

I drop my boys to school, go back home, go straight to bed and sleep again.

~~~~

It's five o'clock in the afternoon, and the math tutor is working with my son. After one hour of working with him, the tutor comes down and talks to me while my husband is listening from the living room. She says, "He doesn't know the timetable!"

I smile politely and answer, "Of course, he does!"

My husband—angrily, in an annoyed tone, with a touch of 'you are stupid and don't understand anything'—yells across from the other room, "She is saying that he doesn't know about the timetable. That means he doesn't know. Do you get it or not?"

Even though I'm very used to not being noticed or respected, I'm totally shocked by the way he feels free to talk to me in front of the teacher. I pretend that I haven't noticed his hostile and degrading tone in front of the tutor. After all, I'm an expert at pretending that everything is ok and nobody saw or heard anything. The tutor keeps up the same pretence as I.

I walk the tutor to the door and say goodbye. I close the door, and I feel I'm turning into something that even I feel afraid of.

My face is all red with an indescribable anger. I'm ready to kill, ready to rip his mouth apart once and for all.

I walk toward the living room, while seeing the image of myself standing by the door with all my suitcases ready.

I step into the living room, force myself to stand still for two seconds, just to be able to control my body. I roar, "Who the hell do you think you are? You have no right to speak to 'me' like that!"

I scream from the top of my lungs. He is totally surprised by my reaction and answers, "Why are you so upset? I didn't say anything bad!"

Still on fire, I continue, "You are like those stinky guys who don't notice their own bad body odour because they are so used to it. But that doesn't mean you don't stink. You are revolting! But listen to me very carefully! You *will not* speak to me like this anymore! Do you get it?"

I think, "A piece of bread and cheese is all I need to live by, and I do *not* need to tolerate all this for it. I can do very well all alone. I can do better without this."

He looks away, pretending that he isn't listening.

~~~~

I walk upstairs, while hearing, "A True and Honourable human being is the One whom Others are safe from—his Words and his Doings."

I remember those millions of times I have done the exact same thing to others, especially in the recent years. I've done it to every single housemaid I have had. To correct them in front of others, sometimes combined with harsh words and a vile tone, did not seem to be a problem for me either.

Hard to admit, but maybe I wasn't raised well either!

Not to correct and criticise someone openly is a basic rule of etiquette in relationships, let alone doing it with a harsh and hostile tone.

~~~~

I am sitting on my bed and still shaking from what took place a few minutes ago. I feel drained and exhausted. The word "connection" comes to my mind immediately…

~~~~

I lose myself in the sound of the drizzling rain, the muddy ground, the smell of the moist soil mixed with the burned wood in the air. I hear the singing sound of the chirping sparrows, and see the graceful rays of the sun, well-hidden behind the clouds and trees in the early hours of the morning.

I think, "It smells like mud! Why does my face feel wet? What is it? My drool? Rain? Water?"

I feel a slight burning pain on the right side of my face as I attempt to lift my head that feels like it weighs a ton. I lift my head, and the drizzle of the rain, combined with the breeze, touches my skin. I notice two wrinkled hands, covered with scratches and bruises, moving toward my shoulders to help me up. I feel a warmth on my right shoulder, spreading all over my body. I spot worry in his dark brown eyes, before I see all the wrinkles on his face.

I think, "He looks familiar. Who is this guy?"

He asks, "Are you ok?"

"I'm fine! Where am I?"

For some odd reason, I can't ask him who he is!

"You are home!"

"Home?"

He has long brown hair and is wearing a long, white kimono. With his concerned and soft voice, he says, "You fell!"

I try to stand up. I'm dressed in a long white dress, a white shawl around my shoulders, my black hair falling on top of my shawl. He is holding my shoulder against his, and, with small steps on the muddy ground, we are walking together.

"Only a few more meters to the steps, my dear!"

I feel the soft touch of my silky dress on my body. The long sleeves are loose. I love this feeling.

I see a blue wooden house. I see the old guy now, holding my white shawl as I walk toward that house.

I think, "I must be dreaming. How did I get here? I must be dreaming. Or am I dead? He said I was home. What did he mean? Who is he?"

Six steps up and he opens yet another door. I say, "So many doors!"

"Yes indeed!"

We are inside the house. The walls are made of clay, and the door is made of used wood and hand-painted in blue. On the left corner of the room there is a white rocking chair with a baby blue cushion on it. I say, "I feel faint. I need to sit on this rocking chair."

I throw myself on it. It's the only furniture in this room. I think, "I get it now, why babies love to be in a rocking bed. What's happening? It feels ok to be here in this house. I feel safe."

I love the smell of the wood combined with the cawing of the crows in the midst of the slightly cold, yet pleasant, surroundings.

I love this déjà vu-like feeling. I remember that I've always wanted to live in a place like this. This place seems like my auntie's wooden house, where I had my best times during my childhood.

I hear the sound of the water from afar and the whistling sound of crickets on the fig trees close by. A dog barks, and the neighbour's dogs bark back. I think, "Really? I live here?"

I turn my head toward the blue wooden door, through which the old guy left the room while saying, "I'll be back with your usual drink."

"Usual drink? I have a usual drink?"

Sitting in the rocking chair, thinking, stirring, looking into nothing, I wonder, "What am I doing here? What is happening? Where is this place?"

The room is lit only with a small lantern. There seems to be no electricity in this house. I get up, hold the lantern in my hand, noticing my own shadow on the wall, and I go outside the room to the veranda. The sound of crickets is echoing everywhere.

I say, "I have to sit. What's happening? What am I doing here? I know this place. Where is everybody? What's happening? Where are my children? Am I dreaming all this? Where is my husband?"

He looks at me with no expression on his face and hands me the pomegranate juice that he's prepared for me in a tall glass.

~~~~

Now, I'm in bed, seeing myself thinking about the name of the 'connection' I wanted to reside in after I came up, post yelling at my husband.

I wonder, "What did just happen? Did I fall asleep for a second? No, I'm sure I didn't. What was this then? Who was this guy? Where was that place I was in, just a moment ago? What just happened?"

I'm completely puzzled. It feels like I just saw a movie that was one hour long in less than a second!

Sunday Again

I feel very lazy and groggy today. I am not sure if I want to go to my "knowing yourself" classes today. Although I feel on top of the world, remembering what happened and the way I stood up for myself yesterday, something that I haven't done before, I still feel shaky inside from time to time.

Overall, it feels like *I* am dissolving, and it's a very uncomfortable feeling.

Sometimes I feel light and happy, but during the same day, my mood swings to the other extreme. I'm still hyper sensitive to noise and, mostly, I feel like going to my room and closing the door behind me. But that disturbing voice about the balcony and the knife does not seem to be bothering me anymore, and it feels like it's gone.

I think, "Let me call my swan lady and see if she wants to go to the gathering today."

She says, "Come and have breakfast with me before we go to this class! What do you think?"

I answer, "Sure! Who could say no to breakfast in your home?"

My swan lady feels like home for me. We eat breakfast in her balcony and speak about this and that, here and there.

One Hour Later

We go to the class, and the teacher is just about to let everyone close their eyes and intend for "connection."

Pleased after the breakfast and the conversation with my friend, with closed eyes, I say, 'connection!'

A few seconds pass. I feel annoyed and think, "What am I doing? This is ridiculous! I can't see anything. I can't feel anything. It's only darkness here. I'd rather have my eyes open and go back to my friend's house and continue eating."

Deeply engaged with all these thoughts, I start to feel cold. My whole body feels like ice.

"Oh my God! What is this?"

I see a tall guy who says he died in a car accident. He looks scared, and he says he doesn't want to go towards the light that is shown to him. I feel very uncomfortable, and I open my eyes. My teacher notices that something is happening to me. With her eyes, she asks if I'm ok.

Shaky and ice-cold, I say, "I'm freezing. I think I'm dead. Could I get a glass of water please?"

With a smile on her face, as if she knows exactly what's happening, she hands me a glass of water. I already feel much better.

The rest of the time, the teacher speaks about the oneness of the universe and the oneness of all that there is.

My head is spinning again with all these fine and unfamiliar words. I close my eyes and lay on the couch, assuring everyone—who were looking at me nervously—that, "I just need to lay down and close my eyes a little. I'm getting sick!

My eyes are closed, and I can't help but hear, "You were on top of everything. You got married for the second time. You changed from an independent, vibrant woman to someone who was ignored like an unwanted guest, silenced like a badly-behaved dog. What happened? How could you step into that role again? Why did you agree to all the mistreatment by putting your head down?

"Why? What happened to that strong personality that freed herself once from a destructive relationship? What happened to that strong woman who moved to a new country all alone to start afresh? Why has this marriage of yours, that was based on love, turned into a nightmare for you? What threw you into that ditch again?"

Short of breath, gasping for air, while holding my chest, I sit up, completely shaken. I just want to run and get out of this place...

Late That Evening

I dare to think about what happened and what I heard earlier today. All my life, I've been my own worst enemy. I have done what others wanted me to, while not feeling happy about it. I have hated what was expected from me, and yet I have done it.

No one cared if I didn't like what I was doing for them, but they didn't care. My sister didn't care. My husband didn't care. No one gave a damn!

I was waiting for others' 'ok' signs. I was waiting for others to say, "Oh, you poor thing! You don't like this? No need to do it!"

I guess this is the way it works. This is the norm. It's sad to acknowledge this hard truth, but this is the way it happens.

> *When self-worth and self-love are lacking, you let others take over the driver's seat of your life.*

The Rise

Discharge

To really know yourself comes with a high price. You need to be ready to do some inner housecleaning first.

If you are not ready to do that, which no one ever is, yet you agree to reside in one of the 'links of connections,' then whether you want it or not, inner housecleaning starts for you anyway.

It will be completely out of your hands. Your body *will* have to—and does—shake off all the garbage parts that your being has absorbed since birth, sometimes even right before birth.

~~~~

"Rebecca! Everything is alright. The MRI is showing that everything is ok!"

I'm feeling ok, but I don't dare to say anything as I feel totally stupefied by this whole thing now. I feel totally fine, like normal.

I muse, "What am I going to say now? That I am totally ok? He arranged an MRI for me because everybody thought I was dying. *I* thought I was dying.

"What should I do? Oh my God, I wish that I actually was dying, instead of this quick recovery! Nothing is wrong with me? But then, what happened to me earlier today? Something was happening earlier today. I was dying. I felt like I was dying. I am sure!"

Earlier Today

I was doing yoga and feeling amazingly great with my friends. I decided to go for another yoga session of twenty minutes.

Ten Minutes Pass

My heart is beating too fast. I feel that I have several hearts in my body, and they are all racing at the highest speed possible. I'm taking deeper breaths to calm down my beating heart. I have to sit down and catch my breath. No, sitting isn't helping. I have to lay down on the ground. Suddenly, I feel my whole body turn ice-cold, as if I am slowly dying. Something inside me is ice-cold, and I'm terrified.

My three friends encircle me and look very concerned.

One of them says, "Your face is white!"

Another says, "Maybe your blood pressure dropped."

"Get the salt! Let's put salt in her mouth!"

"Shall we call your husband?"

"Shall we call the ambulance?"

I'm ice-cold, as if already dead, but yet fully aware of everything that's happening around me. I want to answer, but I'm afraid that if I strain myself, I'll just break and turn off.

I see myself standing in deep dirty mud, and it seems that the level of dirt is rising up. It's a scary scene because soon I will drown in it, I think.

I hear, "All this dirt is rising up to go away because you've asked for it. You collected all these every time you were sad, angry, worried, or disappointed, or when someone else got into a negative state caused by you, knowingly or unknowingly."

I open my eyes and notice one of my friends is putting salt in my mouth by twisting a salt shaker.

My phone rings, it's my husband. I think, "Maybe he felt something, and therefore, he's calling."

I force myself to answer. He sounds stressed and says, "You *have* to go one day and sort out the colour of the doors of the villa. Let's not delay this!"

I say ok repeatedly, in a low voice, trying not to use too much of my energy. I feel that one wrong move and one overly-strong word out of my mouth will turn off the light of my life forever. I'm hanging by a thread that feels as thin as a hair.

Two more minutes pass, and I feel like something is dropping inside me, as if I'm falling apart from inside. It feels like being dropped down from a very high place. I still feel as if I'm dying.

Still on the floor, feeling frightened, I hold my friend's hand and beg her quietly, "Please do not leave me. Just stay with me."

One says, "We have to call the ambulance. Shall we call him and tell him? Why didn't you tell him that you aren't feeling good, darling? You are not getting better. We have to do *something*. Shall we call?"

I nod!

Within minutes my husband is here and a few seconds later, the ambulance guys too.

Suddenly, I start feeling much better, but am taken to the hospital for observation anyway. In the ambulance, I feel embarrassed, thinking, "What happened? What was it that I was experiencing? Why is it gone now? Why am I going to the hospital now?"

I remember when I was feeling ice-cold on the floor, I repeatedly heard a guy's voice, and I could see his face and his naked, handicapped body. He kept saying, "You are dying! Be afraid! I was also always afraid of dying. You are just about to die. You are afraid. Don't move! You should be afraid! You will break soon! Life isn't worth living. I wanted to have a good life and be happy too, but as you can see, I was handicapped. I've been making sure that you don't feel happy either."

Terrified, I had asked him, "Who are You?"

"I'm Tom. It has been a pleasure being with you for a long time since you know very well how to be miserable too."

I think I'm going totally nuts. The chilling memory of what happened is giving me goosebumps. I feel safe now, and my body—although still a bit shaky—feels like it's back to normal.

The feeling of dying has gone, but I'm consumed with the feeling of shame, as I walk out of the ER with my husband's arm around my shoulders.

Something happened to me, and I'm sure it wasn't only physical, although my body was definitely and completely taken by it. I could distinctly feel several hearts beating inside my body. I could surely feel the heavy breathing of 'handicapped Tom.' It made me breathe heavily at times too. Seems like he had taken up residence in my body because he didn't want to leave, because he liked to stay with me.

I still can't believe that I saw all this so clearly, just like a movie. I am familiar with this kind of thing, since we speak frequently about the existence of two different types of non-organic entities in our class, but I have never truly believed it up until now.

I feel more scared than ever. Is someone, who has been dead for a long time, inside me right now? And is he controlling my mind and me, making me think and act in a certain way? Knowing this now is terrifying at so many levels.

~~~

We are home. My husband doesn't ask me anything. He is good at not asking. That's good. Because I don't know how I will answer his question anyway.

I am exhausted and wondering about what happened to Tom. I wonder, "Is he still with me? Or is he gone? Are there others?"

I go to my bed and close my eyes. I intend to reside in that special link of connection that helps one get rid of these unknowingly self-invited guests in one's body temple. I struggle to fall asleep as the shifting of ice-cold to burning-hot feeling repeatedly takes over my body…

In the Wooden House Again

It is dark. I feel like going for a walk. I take the lantern and a step out of the door. The smell of burned fuel reminds me of something pleasant, but right at this instant, I'm not sure from where. Oddly, I feel safe with this smell of burned fuel.

I step outside. It is still raining. Carefully, I walk down the stairs. I'm barefoot, and I feel the wet mud under my naked feet. I look up and see the old guy holding another lantern, standing right there and looking at me. I'm surprised to see him. He seems to be everywhere I go.

He asks, "Going for a walk? I'll join you and show you the way."

I nod and think, "I love this place. If I was to die right at this moment, I wouldn't mind at all as I'm experiencing total safety and satisfaction."

I hear the sound of the rain in the heart of the night. I hear, alongside, the sound of the river accompanied by the singing of the crickets. It's such a delightful symphony to listen to. I absolutely adore it. I want nothing else when I hear this. I'm one with all of this.

He says, "You see?"

I'm puzzled, and think, "How does he know what I am thinking?"

He asks, "Are you sure you want to do this? So soon?"

"Do what? I just want to walk around a little. Do you know what's happening to me? Tell me please!"

He lifts the lantern, looks at me and smiles. I'm too exhausted to argue. I just walk with him as I feel very safe with him.

We pass the handmade wooden bridge. I feel a familiar, slight wiggle when walking on it. I see the muddy water running through the river underneath the bridge. I turn my head and see him stepping on the bridge as well. I ask him, "What's your name? Why am I here? What's this place? Why do I feel drugged? Please tell me."

He answers, "Because you wanted to come here!"

"I don't understand! I need to sit down. I feel dizzy again. I have to sit!"

Passing the man-made bridge, I bend my knees, hold the ground with one hand, and help myself sit on the wet ground. I cry, asking him, "What do you mean?"

He continues, "We have many neighbours. I think you may want to visit them soon."

He points to all the lights, not very far away. Many neighbours, many lit windows.

"Do I?"

I see a crowd standing on the side of the bumpy road to the neighbours.

He says, "Don't worry about them for now!"

I feel faint and reach for the old guy's hand.

"I think I'm dying! I'm very afraid. Please, help me!"

"Yes, you are dying, and you must die!"

Not Little Anymore

Suddenly, I notice that my boys are all grown. I feel like I'm being checkmated by life, by my husband, by me.

I'm consumed with dissatisfaction and anger, and I feel like killing *everyone* who stopped me from cherishing every moment with my children while they were little. Now they are older, and I will never get that precious time back. And this makes me sad and mad at the same time.

It strikes me that I myself killed every moment by being too busy worrying about everybody's demands, all the time. I was too busy trying to show everyone that I'm a superwoman who can take everybody's misery away by trying to straighten and pave the road for them selflessly.

I'm left with this feeling of bitterness over all the lost time.

I missed all those moments, and no one around me was, or is, even one inch more satisfied about me, themselves and life in general anyway. What a waste! I feel cheated. I feel like a person who has sold everything precious at a throwaway price and only now has understood the loss—all those precious moments that will never, ever, ever come back. What a terrible, shameful, hurtful loss.

Intruder

Waking up in the middle of the night, I feel like a giant cube. My attention is toward the centre of it, as if someone is telling me over and over again, "The centre of the cube, the centre of the cube!"

I see many cubes attached to this giant cube. I know that I know something. It feels like I know something about this, but I don't know what it is that I know, yet I'm certain that I know something. That something—I don't know what it is, at least not yet!

Once again, my attention goes to the centre of the giant cube, and I feel a sharp pain inside my chest when, simultaneously, it feels like something drops to a place deep inside me.

I fall asleep again.

~~~~

I am lying on the marble floor in my living room. My helper announces, "You have visitors!"

Two grown women and two young boys rush in. I'm still on a mattress on the floor, wearing my nightgown. I'm very annoyed by this bold and unexpected visit. Their boys are already playing with my children. I rush upstairs to change, and when I return, I see my living room is fully taken over by the two mysterious and intruding women.

Some sort of dark brown fabric has been spread out on the table, which isn't in harmony with the rest of the colours in my home. These women seem very comfortable in my home, and they aren't noticing my annoyance at all. I explode.

"Stop right away and leave my house!

"I don't remember inviting you in. I haven't given you permission to do what you are doing now. Leave at once!"

Looking surprised by my loud voice, they start to put their things together.

I wake up!

I realise that I've been dreaming. I remember the whole dream as if it was something that happened for real! I'm left with a peculiar feeling—relieved and empowered—but I feel like I'm not finished yet. I need to tell the intruders a few more things.

I think, "I want to go back to sleep. I need to do this. I need to tell them a few more things before I'm done."

I struggle to stretch myself back into that zone, to catch the dream. Finally, with closed eyes, I manage to catch the women back in my living room again. This time, I tie them and their boys with a rope. I call the police, put the intruders outside my home and tell them, "You can't just come here and do whatever you want anymore. Get out of my life! Get out of my body! I won't let you control my life any longer."

I slam my door shut with all my power.

Now I open my eyes again, feeling high, feeling like flying this time. I'm free from these intruders, finally, once and for all. I recall struggling so many times with this in my actual life, where people would allow themselves to do just whatever they liked in my home, without caring about my privacy. This time, though, I have finally made it happen. I feel free, stretching in my bed. I feel thrilled thanks to this victory.

I put on my dark blue satin robe and go downstairs for my breakfast.

The ringing of the home phone distracts me for a moment from my grilled cheese sandwich. I think, "Oh, this must be mom! I'll call her back after my last bite."

As soon as I'm done with my breakfast, I press redial, thinking that I'm calling my mother, but I notice that it's not my mom's voice.

I hear my older sister's voice. I shy away from telling her that I didn't actually want to talk to her. I just continue pretending that I meant to call her.

We make small talk. I detect from her tone that she's not happy talking to me.

I can hear that familiar tone, reprimanding me for my choices that she isn't happy with. Unfortunately, somehow, I can even see her face and unhappy demeanour.

After a few minutes of small talk, we say 'goodbye.'

I hang up the phone, and I don't feel like calling mom anymore. Something is bothering me now. The feeling of euphoria I felt a few minutes ago is totally gone. I feel sad, and tears are already all over my face. I thought that I freed myself from the intruders earlier today! But I see another intruder is waving at me right at this moment. Something inside me still crumbles when I say 'No' to others. I know I'll do what I like, but something is still pinching me.

This 'pinching within' is what bothers me now.

I am bothered by the fact that my sister's disapproval of the way I like to live my life these days, which shows up in the tone of her voice, impacts me, troubles me and bothers me.

The real intruder is the one who exists in me—the one who still cares.

Oh my God! I need ropes! I need to call the police again. There is another giant package that needs to be tied up and put outside of me.

I, the Teacher

Even though I have no intention of teaching, I have obtained the requirements necessary for teaching others about Interuniversal Mysticism, the "knowing yourself" classes.

I'm asked by friends to conduct the classes for them. This comes as a total surprise to me as I myself still don't know what I'm doing, and I see myself as a total mess in all levels of my own life.

I try to send the eager students to someone else in town, hoping that they won't ask me again and leave me alone with my messy self.

In the end, I had no choice but to accept as they wouldn't stop asking.

~~~~

On Autopilot

These days, even when I don't close my eyes and do not intend to reside in any of those suggested 'links of consciousness,' I seem to still merge into unexplainable experiences.

In the Wooden House Again

I wonder, "What neighbours was he talking about? Maybe I should knock on the door of one of these houses. I could ask for a glass of water. Maybe they will tell me what's happening around here."

I'm barefoot, rushing, walking toward the neighbours, looking back and making sure the old guy isn't there.

I love the muddy feeling under my feet. I stop for a second, stretching and feel the fresh air in every fibre of my body. I feel like flying as I hear the chirping of the birds in every cell of me, spreading warmth all over me, and the rays of the sun, so kind and gently kissing my face.

When passing the wiggly bridge, holding the long wooden handle, I feel like kissing and smelling it, as if it was a newborn baby, with its new-born-baby smell, hard to resist. I think, "I don't remember the last time I felt so great. Actually, I have never felt this great in my whole life!"

Today, I feel as if the walls, the doors, the stairs, and the lizards are all talking to me.

I hear a voice somewhere within, "If you really look, you will see. If you really listen, you will hear."

This poem of Rumi is whispered out to me,

All the particles of the world
In a hidden way
Talking to you all days and all nights
We all can hear and see and are conscious
Only with those who do not know this, we are silent...

While walking, I see the rays of the sun shining through the dancing leaves and branches of trees all around. The trees seem like giant creatures holding their hanging leaves by thin branches, moving dance-like with the help of the gentle breeze. Mesmerised by this scene, I smile and think, "Oh my God! These trees are speaking."

I feel they are telling me, "Come, Come, Come! Just come this way!"

As if I'm choice-less, I keep walking toward the trees, and I see the first door to the first neighbour. I get the urge to skip this one and go a bit further to the next one, since I am enjoying my flirtation with all these trees.

Before I can even decide whether to stay or continue walking, I find myself knocking on the first door. I wait a little and knock again since no one is opening the door.

I ask, loudly, "Anyone home?"

And think at the same time, "Maybe I should continue walking to the next neighbour anyway."

Just as I'm about to turn, I hear, "Come in!"

I step in cautiously! And am almost shocked by what I see.

I see myself sitting by a silver-coloured door. The door looks cold. It looks like a giant refrigerator door. I seem to be naked, sitting on the floor, holding my knees and my face touching the cold silver giant door. I see myself pressing my face hard against the cold door and crying. I hear myself crying and mumbling, "I need to get in! I need to be near her. I have to stay with her."

Completely shocked by now, with this 'out-of-body experience' scene, I still don't get what's happening.

"Where is the neighbour? What is this? Am 'I' the neighbour?"

I hear, "You need to speak to yourself!"

I turn my head and see the old guy standing behind me. Nervously, I say, "I didn't notice you were here. Please help me! Tell me what's happening? Why am I seeing myself? Why am I naked? Am I dreaming? Why don't I wake up? Why am I so sad? What is this giant door?"

He answers, "This is the door of a morgue."

"Morgue?! Why am I naked and sad? Why am I outside the door of this morgue?"

"You still don't remember?"

"Remember what?"

"Come! Let's go to the next door. You'll understand."

I follow him. It's only a few meters' walk to the next door. I step in, but I don't see a room as I was expecting. I see myself again, but this time I'm digging rectangular shaped holes with my bare hands. I see many packed objects, wrapped in white sheets, lying around.

Terrified I ask, "Am I digging graves? Are these wrapped things bodies? Who are these corpses?"

The old guy looks at me and says, "They are all you!"

I am terrified by what I have just heard, and I cry, "What? What do you mean? What do you mean they all are me?"

I look at him again and tell him, "I feel faint."

He says, "Maybe we should go back? We can walk back if you want. Maybe it's enough for today. Let's go back!"

He takes my hand and gently pulls me toward himself, and I do not resist. Halfway through, on the road to the wooden house, though, I stop.

"I need to see! I need to know! What do you mean? You have to tell me! I need to see. I need to know why I was digging those holes."

~~~~

I run back, and the old guy is running after me. We reach the second door again. I don't knock this time. I just barge in. This time, I dare to go closer to the 'me' who is digging the holes in the ground.

Determined, I ask myself, "Tell me what's happening. Who are all these corpses?"

She answers angrily, "These are all dirt. They have no purpose anymore. Don't worry! They all had to die, and, now, they have to be buried, once and for all. Come! Help me put in the most problematic one first. Do you want to give me a hand?"

"Most problematic one?"

"Yes! The blind and the deaf one of course! The one who couldn't see the truth. The one who didn't know her strength. The one who couldn't see how able she was."

I start crying, "Couldn't see?"

"Yes!"

I'm still weeping, "But why do we need to kill and bury? It all seems so horrible!"

She looks in my eyes for a few seconds as if she wants to find the right words, and eventually says, "Because these are what you mistakenly have been thinking to be 'You'!" Come and help me bury this miserable blind and deaf thing! She isn't serving any purpose anymore. She had to die, and now, she needs to be buried!"

"Why no more purpose? What do you mean?"

"Because the one who can see and hear is born already. There is no place for this blind and deaf one. Come! Let's bury her!"

I take a step forward, bend down and open the white cloth around the area of the head of the first corpse.

Tears flow out uncontrollably from my eyes. It's me. There is no mistake! I weep louder, "Wait a little! Please wait! I need to talk to her first before we put her in the grave."

Howling like a wounded wolf, I say, "I'm so sorry that you had to endure so much pain."

Then I help my 'other' self to lift my own corpse and put it in that ready grave.

With my bare hands, I pour soil over my own corpse.

After the first grave is completely covered, I need to sit down again. I say, "We need to wait a little!"

"Ok!"

I sit on the wet ground again. The tears roll down, almost drowning my face. Between sobs, I manage to ask, "Was I really blind? I could see 'her' eyes before we put 'her' inside the grave."

"Totally blind to see and utterly deaf to hear clearly about the purpose of your life. You were blind to see the grandness of yourself, blind to see what everyone else saw in you and deaf to hear all the good everyone else said about you."

I wonder, "Who was everyone?"

"Blind to see what the taxi driver in LA saw and deaf to hear what he actually told you that day when you wanted to go to the Metropolitan Motel. Blind to see what the old Danish patient saw, deaf to hear what she was actually trying to tell you that day in the hospital. Everything and everyone spoke in so many ways, but you weren't able to hear and see."

I think for a moment, and then argue, "I actually heard everything everyone ever said to me. I heard a little too well, listened too well. What do you mean?"

"Yes, you listened very well to everything that was negative, everything that wasn't true."

I pause, sigh and answer, "Maybe!"

With sadness in my heart and in my eyes, I admit, "I listened only too well to everybody's destructive comments about me, but I didn't hear when someone told me the good. I forgot—over and over again—that I was perfectly able. I thought I needed those people's approval in my life."

I continue sitting there a few minutes, gazing at the freshly-covered grave in front of me. I sigh again, "I buried myself! I buried my most destructive self."

I get up and start walking toward the blue wooden house. Straightened up, I take slow and gentle steps, looking at the trees with their dancing branches. I don't look back. I don't look for the old guy.

I think, "I need to be left alone with myself. I need some rest!"

I reach the wooden house. I go in and sit in the rocking chair and wrap my white shawl around me. I am thoughtful. I'm tearful. My head is pounding. A world of thoughts is rushing in my head.

I hear, "Look closer! You need to look closer!"

Guy in Cinnabon Shop

A bald guy in his thirties stands too near to me in the queue. I ask him, "What are you doing?"

He yells, "What am I doing? I'm standing in line to buy a Cinnabon!"

I think, "He stands so close to me, and now he is rude and yelling."

I turn back look at him and say angrily, "Back the hell up before I call the police, so they make you understand that you shouldn't stand so close next to a lady!"

He becomes quiet and looks concerned. It looks like he suddenly remembers that he is living in a Muslim country, that he is a Muslim himself and that his behaviour is to be questioned according to Islamic values.

I get my Cinnabon, sit down, and get busy eating with my

boys. I lift my head and am eye to eye with the bold guy I just told off completely.

I can't help but see what his eyes were saying, "I made a mistake standing too near to you in the queue, and I made a mistake yelling when you asked what I was doing, but I didn't mean to stand too close to your body in a malicious way. You were absolutely wrong about me."

I frown, pinched by this seeing and hearing. I think, "All my collected fury from my childhood, the neighbour guy and the insults from many others came to life in the shop, and I lashed out at this guy. He's an ill-behaved person because he doesn't understand personal space, sure. But maybe he didn't mean it."

I feel guilty.

That Evening

I am still thinking about what happened earlier today. A strong voice inside me tries to convince me that I didn't do wrong. I hear, "What you sense is never lying. Do you really think that guys, too close to your body, bring you to this feeling of disgust? Are you really sure about this?

"What about that old guy in that nursing home that you took for a walk every day? He was eighty years old. Remember? You held him tight. You walked with him. You didn't feel disgusted. Remember! Your intuition is never wrong."

The voice makes sense. I recall not feeling disgusted, unsafe, or anything out of the ordinary with so many guys that I encountered and who had stood close to me.

But I continue to feel horrible about this whole incident. I feel I haven't evolved one bit and still am that bitter and wounded girl who likes to tell people off, instead of giving them the benefit of the doubt. I decide I don't want to teach 'Knowing Yourself' classes anymore as I feel I'm not worthy of teaching things I can't yet practice myself...

Prison

I'm in jail, visiting someone. Oh my God! I see that it's Dr Taheri. I have never met him in person, but he smiles at me as if he knows me. He says, "Come in! Sit with me. I have nothing to do here either. We could write together!"

I ask, "Do you know who I am?"

He smiles again, shows me a paper and says, "Yes, of course! And this is your signature. I know very well who you are!"

I answer, "I can't come in. I can't stay. I don't want to stay. I'm not good enough. I'm leaving and not coming back!"

I start to walk away. He runs after me, alongside the tall fences of the prison yard. It seems that he can move freely. He stops me and says, "Please, please, please, don't go away! Please don't go away! Just stay!"

I stop and look at him for a moment. I walk with him into his cell. He shows me a book and silently points to the title.

He looks at me, making sure that I see the title that reads, *Reconciliation*.

~~~~

I wake up and know for sure that I *must* continue teaching the classes. I can't think about anything else but the word 'Reconciliation.'

What does it mean to reconcile with all that there is? I know what it means but don't understand it. To reconcile with others? How is it possible? With the knowing of the whole picture, the connectedness of everything? All I know is about fighting. I know it by heart, because I was trained well this way throughout my life.

Only recently, I've learned how to show everyone where the lines are—my lines, my boundaries. I've thrown whoever doesn't respect my boundaries out of my life. I've gotten rid of them, and it feels fantastic. I know now how to separate myself from others. But what is the meaning of reconciliation with others?

A memory flashes from many years ago. Fifteen years ago, we gathered together as a family, my two sisters, their families and my mom in my home. The good time that we were supposed to have turned into many "whys." Why has no one ordered my favourite sandwich? Why did he mention what was missing on the dinner table? Why is he so sour all the time?

There were two weeks of juggling constantly with all these whys, that finished with the biggest and the funniest why of all. My mother scored the highest by asking, "Why did we gather together at all? Someone tell me! *Whose* idea was that we gather together at all?"

She said it with an angry and annoyed expression on her face that was serious but also very funny, as if she was ready to beat up the person who had suggested this gathering.

Maybe my mom is the cause for the element of separateness among humanity! Because she was, in fact, saying, let's stay far away from each other so that we don't notice that we actually don't like each other and that we can't tolerate each other at all!

That's how she knew how to maintain peace around her. That's how I've learned how to maintain peace—by staying separate physically and emotionally.

But I want to know how to reconcile with the world and with people. At this stage, even though I don't want to, something in me knows that I ought to.

~~~~

I'm on the spinning bicycle at the gym and spinning away in my mind with the loud music. I feel that I'm flying, and I suddenly find myself on my bicycle on that rainy day in Copenhagen when I was hurrying to work. It's a rainy grey day with a little bit of sunshine. I take a deep breath of the fresh and cold air. Many memories flash forward, and I feel dizzy. Everything's spinning now.

I see everything from the beginning in an orderly manner. I see that I have always been equally 'good' and equally 'bad.' I see the balance of it all. I see everything there is in this life like in a fish tank, where everything is affecting everything else at the same time.

I see it all. I see the look. I see the slap. I see the VCR day. I see the look of ridicule. I see myself talking too much, explaining too much. I see the worried one. I see the scared one. I see all the infidelities I committed toward myself. I see the mute one. The one who waits to be rescued all the time. The dependent one! The nervous talker! The always available one! The martyr! The complaining master. The offended master. The victim master. The restless one. The always tired one. The explosive one. The ugly one. The weak one. The insecure one. I see the disrespectful one.

And I Find Myself in the Wooden House...

I see myself running, crying, gasping for air.

"I need to go back."

I stumble on the ground and find myself rubbing my arms

and my body with my shawl, as if trying to wipe some dirt off me. Completely out of myself, out of breath, my head is pounding, my face is red, my eyes flamed.

I think, "I need to get to her again. I need to help her. I need to dig more graves. We need more graves. I will dig all of them with my own bare hands. I need to do this. Oh my God, I have to bury them. I need to get there as fast as I can."

I reach the second door, the second neighbour. I push the door wide open. I'm stunned by what I see and scream, "What? What's happening? Where are all the graves? Where is my other me?"

Still completely out of myself, still not breathing entirely, eager to dig more, and yet, disappointed. My head is still pounding, my face is even redder, and my eyes more flamed.

Suddenly, I see the old guy appearing out of nowhere and standing there and watching me.

"Where is she? Why is this place empty? Where is she? What happened?"

He answers, "Let's go to the next door!"

"Why? Is she there, do you think? I need to do this. I need to bury a few. I need to dig with my bare hands. I need to do it now, now, now!"

He looks calm and says, "I know! Let's walk a little. Let's walk a bit further to the next door."

He takes me out toward the next door. When we reach, I kick the door and am totally stunned with whom I see. I cry out, "What are you doing here, darling? Oh, I'm sorry! I didn't mean to say it like this. I'm happy to see you. Oh, I'm so happy to see you!"

My swan lady is sitting on a single light green sofa, smiling at me, and says, "Hi angel! Come on in!"

I sit on the floor, exhausted, looking at her. Not able to stand up, I drag myself in a crawl toward her and put my head on her lap. I burst out, "I did it. I did all those things myself. I allowed it. I let it happen, and others didn't hesitate. I believed them. I need to die. I know it now."

My swan lady tearfully, yet lovingly, listens to this totally broken me who is cracking open like this for the first time. I grab my friend's skirt, almost out of breath now, with puffy eyes, sobbing, "I told everyone that they could do whatever they wanted. I let it happen. I became what I hated. I got the same bad smell. I let others do it to me, and others let me do it to them. It's so sick!

"Why did I let them? Because I was used to it. I believed what others said to me. Because I knew nothing else.

"I was a good friend despite their sharp tongues, their poisonous comments, and their infected words because deep down I believed their words. I was so damn weak and afraid!"

I see that familiar look in her eyes, the one that I've always loved. That glance in her eyes that made me feel safe with her. In a flash, I remember the breakfast party in my new house. I had invited friends to my home. The day after, she had called me and said,

"Oh my God! Why did you look so tired yesterday? Why?"

She had almost been crying when she said these words. Her tone was caring, gentle and affectionate.

I guess there are reasons why we love some people. It's not what they say, it's *how* they say what they say. It's not what they do, it's *how* they do what they do. These rare people are able to give you 'that' gift of true love and compassion that can't be bought in a store.

She whispers now, "You're wrong! You aren't weak. You aren't worthless. You were always helping others even when you were in a deep mess. That is the quality of a strong person. You just need to wake up!"

I continue sobbing, and say, "They said all those things about me, and that's what I think about myself today. Unfortunately, I still believe what they say. How to get rid of that belief? How to erase all those programs? How can one be strong when one feels weak from within, when the programming screams 'weak' and 'can't do it'?

"I was so miserable so I made sure that everyone around me was miserable too. I would make sure others felt the pain I felt. I caused pain because I didn't want to feel pain anymore. Unfortunately, I remember how I was, and it also bothers me to remember. I hate myself."

Only now I can see how horrible others were to me and, therefore, how horrible I was to Jan and to most other people.

I cry and cry and cry. She's caressing my head all the time. Slightly calmer now and feeling safe, I look at my friend. She is still smiling.

I hear, "No one is guilty, only a bunch of unaware victims entangled with each other. You are not guilty, but you just are one among many sinners. The sin of not knowing. Not knowing who you are and why you are 'here.'"

I pause for a moment. I am still shedding tears, but am much calmer. I get up and walk toward the second door and I enter.

Calmly, I start digging new graves with my bare hands.

I kiss all my old "me's" goodbye.

I especially take my time and look at the ones who were so easily influenced by others.

"You all have to go! I don't want any of you in me anymore!"

I put them in, one by one.

~~~

I get up and want to go back to the wooden house. I need to rest.

The old guy tells me, "Let's go back now. It's enough for today. But 'know' that you are not done yet…"

Aziz Khanoom

It's late at night. A private agency has brought her straight from the airport to us. She is a petite, slightly chubby woman in her late forties. I have just opened the door for her. She introduces herself, and I show her the room.

I am suddenly overwhelmed by an undeniable pain all over my body, deep inside my bones that I can't ignore.

A grown woman, almost my age, arrives in a foreign country, straight to a new home, without knowing who or what is waiting for her. I feel extremely sad for her, and think, "I can't even imagine what it must feel like!"

I offer her something to eat, but she repeatedly says,

"No need! I'm full!"

I don't know why, but I feel very sad in general. After settling her in her room, I find myself talking to Jan in my mind, "Hey! Come and get your last unreceived salary. You just left without getting your salary. Also, I'll pay you for all those presents you had in that suitcase that I angrily threw away."

I think, "I know I was mean to her. I spoke badly and angrily almost all the time. But why were her reactions more violent than my verbal attacks?

"Who knows what horrible and unimaginable things she had to endure all her life? While her cup was easily overflowing at twenty-six, mine was overflowing at forty."

I go upstairs and lay on my bed.

I close my eyes and instantly see flashes of Jan's face smiling at me. She looks very happy, like during those first days she came to us.

I feel comforted to see her so happy, and I just know, for sure, that I am forgiven…

~~~

"Such a Blessing Is This None-Place of No-thingness."

— Shams Tabrizi

I know that I'm dreaming. I'm very excited about attending Dr Taheri's new classes. A big crowd is waiting in the hallway, waiting for him to come in.

I jump forward. He sees me and stretches his right hand to shake my hand. I surprise myself by kissing his hand instead of a normal handshake.

I can see the surprised look in his face, and I can also see that he is worried about my embarrassment, which is inevitably there already.

Totally embarrassed, I walk away from him and try to blend into the rest of the crowd which are waiting there. I am trying to look away and forget about my silly, spontaneous kissing hand outburst.

I turn my head again and am surprised to see him standing next to me, smiling. He puts his right arm around my shoulder, resting his weighing hand on my shoulder.

We start walking a little, and suddenly no one else is around.

He says, "You are exactly like me."

A big door opens, and we both enter.

I'm all alone now, still feeling the heaviness of his hand on my right shoulder.

I see a waterfall that continues joining a river of green and turquoise blue water, mixed with snow-white coloured foam, forcefully, yet elegantly, streaming through middle of the forest next to a green and orange ground.

The light, the water, the sound, the colours—I see all, one by one, and there is no separateness between me and all that I'm observing. I am consumed with a feeling of completeness...

My gaze is on the streaming water. Somehow, I hear the water drops telling me, "Be silent!"

Instantly, I'm reminded of all the million times my husband has told me that I talk too much and need to be quiet. I never got it until now...

I see my tree friends from the wooden house. The cawing of a crow, the bark of the dog, the faint sound of crickets runs through my veins.

I am walking around and feel the wet soil under my bare feet. I'm amazed to know that I 'hear' the soil with my feet.

I look down to see the soil and my feet. I *feel* my feet on the wet soil with my eyes. My eyes 'are' the soil under my feet.

It's dark now, and it's raining. I'm the rain. I'm the drops of rain, and I'm the sound of the rain. In the heart of the night, I'm the darkness of the night and the shimmering light that is hitting the ground.

With my eyes gazing at rain, darkness and the shimmering light, I'm being lifted up into the sky. I get the feeling of being an eagle. I'm flying high, high, high and observing a limitless desert that is stretched infinitely.

Not having enough time to know for sure if I actually am that observing eagle or not, I'm pulled elsewhere.

I'm among a crowd of wild cows. I see hair, unusually thick hair that is covering my eyes.

I notice, "Oh my God! I'm not just watching this. I'm a wild cow myself, among a herd of cows that are moving very, very slowly."

Instantly, I am pulled from this scene, deep into an ocean swimming with other turtles, shifting in less than a second to being an ant and to a small fish above water of another ocean, and now shifting again, into being a lizard or something very small under a bush.

It's dark, and I'm high up in the sky again. I see a colourful city, from a far distance. I want to go down and move toward this magnificent city, but, somehow I'm not able to.

I get the notion and am reminded that I am the eyes that see it all. I am the knowing. And I know that I have already experienced all these experiences and also countless others.

~~~

Now, I see the old guy in front of me. He tells me, "It's time now, to get to know your guests. Remember?"

He walks me through the forest toward the wiggly bridge.

I see that huge crowd again, standing by the bridge, and I hear the murmur of their talk,

"*Fight. Argue. Alone is good. Just by yourself. Quick. Hurry up. Eat. Kill yourself. Everything is wrong. Don't move. Kill yourself. You are useless. What's the point? Kill yourself. Be afraid. Be offended...*"

I'm totally mortified and dizzy. The old guy takes my arm

and leads me into the wooden house.

I see many odd-looking creatures in the room.

Terrified, I scream, "What are these? I didn't see them last time I was here!"

One of the creatures is a giant and is so big that it is almost filling the whole room. It's so huge that its head touches the ceiling.

I'm on the floor, doubled up, in a corner. I wish I could run away, but there is nowhere to go, nowhere to run. I'm so scared to look. I don't know what all these creatures are. I close my eyes very tight. I don't want to see anything. I open my eyes just barely to see if they are gone.

I see a big crowd of people again. They all are looking at me and walking toward me.

The giant says, in a ridiculing voice, "It doesn't really matter if you want to look at me or not. I've been with you for a long time!"

I dare to think, "What do you mean?"

He replies, "I'm controlling most of yours and many other people's thoughts! You have done very good so far, leaving the door open for all of us."

Another creature who looks like a midget, with long hair covering his head, seems to have no face or eyes. He points to the ceiling and says, "Look up! Them too! They have been with you for quite some time, controlling your thoughts!"

I look up and see a black spider and also a tall man in a suit. I can't see his face. I see a woman—a very big-boned one—and a boy dressed in a pirate outfit. One creature is bold—one eye on the right cheek with one tooth.

The old guy says, "You have to get rid of these! Clean up! You left the door open and let them in. You have sinned! Every time you cried, every time you were worried, upset or sad or agitated, you drew these creatures into or around your body temple."

I'm pulled back to that day in my nursing training, in that locked psychiatric unit, where every night, my mentor would say, "Now, we try to maintain a peaceful environment for everyone here…"

I didn't get it then, but finally, after 27 years, I do get what she really meant. I realise that I've violated this basic and fundamental rule only about several billion times in my whole life.

The old guy interrupts my thought, "The purpose of one's life isn't to do so and be in a negative state."

~~~~

Now, I see another big-featured, ugly woman with her sad-looking husband standing silently next to her. It's shown to me that they live in my garden, in my pool, and they even sometimes sleep in our bedroom. As I look at them, the big-featured woman speaks, "I'm the one who is in your mouth, making you talk nonsense and behave not very ladylike sometimes. I've been around for more than 500 years and in your family since 100. I'm the one behind every friend you thought something was wrong with and threw them out of your life. I made sure you were alone. I wanted you to be mine only. I made sure you broke ties with Luis and many others."

I feel a choking sensation in my throat and feel like throwing up.

I hear screaming, the crying voice of a young man. He is naked, and he is being tied up with ropes, like ready to be taken away somewhere. I feel a spreading pain all over my body due to his screaming. He begs me to stay. I can't bear his crying. I close my eyes and remember to reside in that special connection. I command him to leave. He cries loudly, hitting his naked and deformed legs on the ground.

Doubtful and exhausted by hearing him, I think again, "Maybe he can stay for a while…"

I see a movie-like slideshow that shows me how all my stagnation, my never-ending feeling of tiredness, and my playing the victim were all caused by him possessing my mind in my body temple.

Simultaneously, I see a tree surrounded by tiny snowflake-like particles. It is shedding its yellow leaves.

Saddened by all this knowing, I wish I could be thrown into fire, so all these unwelcome entities would burn away. I close my eyes and intend to reside in that special field of consciousness that helps to rid one of all unwelcome entities…

While he is still screaming and crying, I say to him, "Please walk toward the light."

He, and a huge crowd with him, move away from where I am. In parallel, I see that I'm standing in a building, led to go to a different section, but still observing the section I just left. I'm watching the other part of the building being destroyed.

~~~~

I'm shifted to the street, outside the house I grew up in.

I see the fight and hear the screaming of my uncle and aunt, letting all the neighbours know that the ongoing scandal belongs to my family.

In this out-of-body experience, someone stops me and asks, "What's your last name?"

"My last name? What's my name?"

And I see an ugly guy, without teeth, smirking at me. I see

myself, shivering out of fear and shame, in that moment when my uncle is shouting out loud in the street outside our home, "This is the house of...Don't switch off the light!"

The toothless guy smirks and says, "I've loved you since and you have loved 'me' since then. I also hated my last name and hated myself."

The old guy from the wooden house appears and says, "Your last name was scandalised so brutally in your mind, when, in fact, pride of who you are should have been implemented when you were young. And yet, the undeniable fact is that you chose *this* platform, *this* city, *this* family. They needed you, and you needed them. You chose the city of Rasht because this is and has always been the city of strong women. You chose and you landed here, and then, as usually happens to everyone, you forgot all about it."

I see the lady from the wall again, and, once again, I melt seeing her.

She says, "When separating others, your 'thoughts' repeatedly made you believe that it was a sign of weakness. You fell for that trick. You've been totally fooled, and you didn't know that it's always been the exact opposite.

"Only a very strong person could do what you did, trying to separate people when they were fighting.

"You were always strong, not weak at all."

New York

It's night, and I am sitting in the living room. My boys are upstairs and busy playing their games. My husband is watching the news.

It seems to be an ordinary and quiet night, and I'm taking it easy as it has somehow been unusually crazy for me, with all my unfamiliar experiences lately.

I am caught off-guard by a sudden feeling of tremendous sadness which is taking over me totally.

I feel like I miss New York. Strangely, I feel that I just need to be there, and I need to be there now.

I have never lived in New York. I was just there as a tourist last summer, but it was like love at first sight. During those three short days we spent there, I felt a deep connection with that city, and I was in a state of euphoria all the time.

And now, desperate with this tremendous feeling of longing, I try to think about a way that would help me live in this marvellous and alive city.

I think, "I must be there. I must live in New York City, or I will die. But how should I do that? If I move there, where am I going to live? I can't afford living there. I don't have a place to stay. Oh! I know. I could go and live in a shelter for the homeless…"

I smile as I finally find a way to be in the city I am so deeply in love with, and I'm surprised that I am willing to imagine being homeless and living in shelters, just to have the chance of being there.

I feel happy about finding a solution to my 'missing New York' problem.

And as I go to bed, I think, "What is this? Is it me who is experiencing this?

After all my experiences lately, I know now about this truth that, in fact, entities can possess our minds and make us think, speak and act in certain ways.

So, I think further, "What is this I have just experienced? Am I thinking and feeling on behalf of another soul who has lost his or her way? Or am I being reminded of an already experienced experience?"

Finally, Eye to Eye

I notice something!

Something is watching me! I can't see it, but I'm aware that 'it' is watching me.

Surprisingly, it seems that 'something'—that 'invisible eye'—that is watching me is still me!

When I look to detect it, I can't find it, but I *know* for sure that it's me that is looking at me.

All this time, *I've* been the one. The eye that watches me is the eye that I am, and it's the 'I' that discovers everything. That 'I' which knows all.

Suddenly, I hear this song everywhere again,

For that fragrance of your surrounding
In my thought
Without you, I'm aimlessly walking around
It takes me to the moment I'm face to face with you
Your world and the unique feeling
Together with you, only the indescribable

I see and hear the lady from the wall and the old guy from the wooden house, stretching into forever...

"We were behind all, in different ways and through different people,

The smile in the tram,
Those who kissed your hands,

Those who gave you compliments,
The taxi driver,
The Danish patient,
Those who pushed you down
Every harsh and unkind word,

Luis brought back to remind you about your happy years.
Tara brought back to remind you about your vibrant self.

We have always been with you, all the way, to help you wake up.
And we always will be with you."

In a state of awe, I smile.

I see my boys, my husband, Tara, Swan lady, my house, my city, and I am consumed with joy and one thought only, "I have everything. I am exactly where I am supposed to be!"

I find myself thinking of a poem by Rumi,

One's life has come to an end while waiting for that desired paradise
One didn't know that,
To be 'wish-less' is being in that paradise already…

~~~~

I know now.

I'm ready to say goodbye to all my guests now. I see them all in front of me and I say,

"*This* is where you all leave me—those of you who are in me, those who are around me, those who are talking to me and interacting with me through others."

I say goodbye to the men and women, big and small, ugly and beautiful, all the dark ones and deformed ones, the young and the old ones.

Suddenly, I see my dad in front of me, looking at me.

Tearful, I tell him, "Goodbye daddy! You must go too. I don't want your 'upsets' in me anymore. But, before you go, I need to tell you something. You need to know how sorry I am. I was not aware and had no understanding that you were totally destroyed after my 'brother's eye' incident many, many years ago.

"You couldn't help yourself, you were wounded by your grief. You changed and therefore you did all those things that were not you. I understand it now."

One by one, the crowd walks toward a shimmering light from far far away. Some are still crying, begging to stay, and some are still smirking, but the whole bunch is moving toward the light...

Third Time's a Charm

I am traveling to Venice again, and I am very excited.

This time I'm here with an agenda—to wipe away the bad memories of my two previous visits to this magical ancient island and to create new loving memories.

I take the bus to town. I enjoy my walk by the magnificent canals of beautiful Venice. It's cold and cloudy. I enjoy looking at people from all over the world—the gondolas, the souvenir shops, everything.

I'm looking for something, and I can't find it. I'm surprised. It's gone. All the bad memories, that I wanted to replace with good ones, were nowhere to be found. I didn't need to replace anything. Before I travelled to Venice, I had been thinking, "I have unfinished business with the city of Venice. Can't wait to get there, so I can make good memories this time!"

I now wonder, "Where are all my bad memories? I don't remember anything! Although I remember the flying pizza on the wall from my first trip, but it only makes me laugh! No sad memory at all."

Something has changed inside me, and that something feels great.

Played Big Time

I am in the kitchen preparing snacks and watching the TV in the living room. We are watching the video clips of the boys when they were very little. From one birthday to another, the dancing of the boys on our bed, and all their singing moments.

All four of us are watching and laughing. Together. I'm still in the kitchen, laughing and amazed by all these great moments that I filmed and was a part of.

A realisation suddenly strikes me, and I can't hold back my tears. I feel fooled, as the voiceless voice in my head whispers,

"Look! So many good memories you made with your children! Look! How happy they were! Who says you weren't a good mother? Who says you didn't do enough? You were a very, very good mother, and your boys were very happy all the time."

Still tearful and with a huge lump in my throat, I see my younger son kissing my husband. They are both giggling and watching the clip when he was only two. He was jumping on our bed, repeatedly taking off his underwear! I see joy and happiness in moment after moment in those videos. And I see my husband almost everywhere in those clips, being very, very good.

I hear, "Who said he was upset all the time? Who said he wasn't good? Who said that he destroyed all the moments?"

The popcorn and the snacks are ready. I wipe my tears and go over to the living room, enjoying our togetherness one more time.

I Continue to Think

"Something, or somethings, made me think negatively about everything. Something made me see things with a cloud of negativity most of the time. It wasn't all bad. It was all bad seeing and bad whispering in my mind and ears..."

Now I clearly see that more than ninety-nine percent of what has happened in my life has been great.

The Panoramic Understanding

As I have heard Dr Taheri say once,

"Sometimes, it only takes one major thing to be totally observed in our existence. That one 'thing' could be the exact reason behind every destructive behaviour and outcome in one's life..."

What was that thing for me?

I let things, people, and circumstances influence me which led to misery for me and others.

Instead of hearing and being influenced by that stronger inner voice, which has always been nearer to me than the artery of my neck, the voice that I am, the voice that has always been with me and always will be, I was totally overpowered by all my emotional scars. Because of that, I absorbed and attracted those unwanted guests in and around my body temple and let them control my every thought and move.

And above all, I was totally unaware of what Pierre Teilhard de Chardin once said,

"We are spiritual beings having a human experience."

I didn't know that we are infinite and the experience of 'this' life is 'only' one of countless experiences that our souls embark on.

If I had known this before, I would not have taken things so seriously.

~~~~

I understand now, that our soulmates, apart from those wonderful people who bring out the best in us, could also be those who will push our buttons, those who are here to teach us something, those who will do anything to help us wake up.

So if everyone I meet in life is my teacher, soulmate and awakener, and they are—in fact—chosen by me, attracted to me, by me, and by my own initial vibes, then what does it really mean to have grudges toward anybody?

As long as I am not aware of the vastness of my being, my destructive vibrational frequency invites in all the unwanted. What follows is one agonising experience after another as the result. In other words, all the sins of not knowing…

Thanks to this knowledge now, I don't need anybody's apology anymore because I don't hold any grudges toward anyone anymore. On the contrary, I ask for other's forgiveness often, as it makes me lighter to move on…

And I truly feel grateful for all those who were sent my way and those who I attracted myself so they could help me wake up.

~~~~

Ultimately, I know now that I have chosen to be here, to experience new things, and to awaken from the dream of not knowing.

When I get in touch with, and get to know, that very core of my existence, then inevitably, I 'will' know about all that is piled up in me. And as I know myself, I automatically will have understanding for others' seemingly crazy acts too.

Overall, I love this feeling of not needing to ask 'Why' anymore.

As I become aware of my wounds, I see the wounds of others...

Everything, and everyone, becomes so transparent.

All those years of not knowing myself have made me guilty of unfaithfulness toward me and everyone else.

At the same time, I realise that everyone is doing the right thing because they are doing what they do, depending on *their* level of knowing at that given moment.

As learned and experienced so far, we live in a dual world, which means everything gets to be understood by its opposite pole, like good and bad, dark and light, Yin and Yang, etc.

If I let myself constantly be in all the negative states, I simply allow myself to be used by the negative force in this dual life-form, and allow that side of life to use me for its purpose and vice versa...

I also realise that when I don't stand up for myself in life, or for others, I'm responsible for the negative karma that is created. I'm responsible for the unknowing act of that person too, because I didn't stand up and I didn't object. With my fear and silence, I only let them believe they were right to do what they were doing.

As For My Housemaids

My invisible scars, and not being aware about anything, faded my empathic self. I just wanted each of my housemaids to be a super human being, with no life or feelings of their own. My need was for them to make life easy for *me*, especially when I didn't know how to deal with all the pressure, from either inside or outside, that I was enduring.

I became unkind because I didn't feel well.

Unlike today, very little did I know about the connectedness of us all, the law of cause and effect and that 'just' karma.

"All human beings are parts of 'one body'
If one part is hurt by life, the other part won't feel rested."

— Ferdosi, Persian poet

And when I cast a glance over the actions of the majority of people on earth, I notice similar destructive patterns of behaviour more or less everywhere.

I did not know who I was and, likewise, I did not know who everyone else I met was. And so, I did not realise each of us is as vast as the universe.

I was totally unaware that, if I wanted to, with just a flicker of intent, I could have access to countless, already obtained experiences. Like the experience of being high, high in the sky, like an eagle, in one moment. And, in the same moment, observe the (already obtained) experience of being deep in an ocean and swim with many turtles. And so forth.

I was totally unaware that I, as the eye of the observer, could simultaneously see all the already-obtained experiences in a 'no time' and 'no place' zone.

I did not know that I am so much. Therefore, I chose—like many others—to play small.

I am *not* small.

Neither are you.

We are all so much and so able, but just not aware of it yet.

I, like many, many others, simply did not know that, whatever I do in this life, I do it to myself.

As the insightful quote of Dr Taheri suggests,

"Humans have only one problem. None awareness!"

One Thing I Know for Sure,

"True worshiping of God, 'is' to help others…"

— Saadi, Persian poet

Today

"Boys!

Hurry up! Don't forget to brush your teeth, we want to smell fresh when we talk to our friends, right? Go upstairs and kiss daddy-doo goodbye!"

The boys are still sitting and eating, heads in their phones, not in a rush at all.

"Let's move it! Let's move it! Remember I have my four hours talk today at nine o'clock, I have to be back before that."

Everyone is in the car heading to school. I tell the boys about the busy day I have ahead, "Right after my talk, I have to attend the conference call with aunty Tara, prepare your lunch before picking you up, and let's see if swan lady feels like chatting while driving to her job."

I continue, "'Bye boys! Love you! Remember who you are! Kings won't need correcting and reminding! Do your work perfectly. Perfect like you are! Love you guys!"

"Ok! Love you mom!"

And, while driving back, I find myself smiling, "No matter what, my life is good! Knowing that, this is, only one out of the infinite experiences I have had…"

The End

About the Author

Fereshte Gholamalizaden Kasbakhy is a licensed nurse by education and a teacher by life's experiences. She has been a teacher of Interuniversal Mysticism since 2010.

From an early age, she has been an eager seeker for answers to life's most fundamental questions. In pursuit of finding those answers, she attended countless number of psychology and various type of spirituality courses, deeply observed the teachings of Eckhart Tolle, Rupert Spira, Allan Watts, Krishnamurti and countless other spiritual teachers, until she was introduced to the teaching of Dr Taheri's Interuniversal Mysticism.

Fereshte currently lives in the UAE, enjoying life with her husband and their two children. When she's not busy working on her next book, she holds regular meetings and online courses of Interuniversal Consciousness, or can be found reading, writing, camping, or working on her absolute favourite hobby—painting.

To contact the Author, write to:

Email: fereshtekasbakhy@hotmail.com
Facebook & Instagram: Fereshte Kasbakhy

Or

Call: 00971-505336358

Ingram Content Group UK Ltd.
Milton Keynes UK
UKHW020055170623
423582UK00006B/235